FREE VIDEO

Series 7 Essential Test Tips Video from Trivium Test Prep!

Thank you for purchasing from Trivium Test Prep!
We're honored to help you prepare for your exam.
To show our appreciation, we're offering a

FREE *Series 7 Essential Test Tips* Video

Our video includes 35 test preparation strategies that will make you successful on your big exam. All we ask is that you email us your feedback and describe your experience with our product. Amazing, awful, or just so-so: we want to hear what you have to say!

> To receive your FREE *Series 7 Essential Test Tips* Video,
> please email us at **5star@triviumtestprep.com**.

Include "Free 5 Star" in the subject line and the following information in your email:

1. The title of the product you purchased.
2. Your rating from 1 – 5 (with 5 being the best).
3. Your feedback about the product, including how our materials helped you meet your goals and ways in which we can improve our products.
4. Your full name and shipping address so we can send your *FREE Series 7 Essential Test Tips DVD*.

If you have any questions or concerns please feel free to contact us directly at:
5star@triviumtestprep.com.

Thank you!
– Trivium Test Prep Team

Series 7 Exam Prep 2024-2025:

4 Practice Tests with
Detailed Answer Explanations
[7th Edition]

Elissa Simon

Copyright ©2023 by Trivium Test Prep

ISBN-13: 9781637989463

ALL RIGHTS RESERVED. By purchase of this book, you have been licensed one copy for personal use only. No part of this work may be reproduced, redistributed, or used in any form or by any means without prior written permission of the publisher and copyright owner. Trivium Test Prep; Accepted, Inc.; Cirrus Test Prep; and Ascencia Test Prep are all imprints of Trivium Test Prep, LLC.

The Financial Industry Regulatory Authority, Inc. (FINRA) was not involved in the creation or production of this product, is not in any way affiliated with Trivium Test Prep, and does not sponsor or endorse this product. All test names (and their acronyms) are trademarks of their respective owners. This study guide is for general information and does not claim endorsement by any third party.

Image(s) used under license from Shutterstock.com.

Table of Contents

Introduction vii

1 **Practice Test** 1

Answer Key 17

2 **Practice Test** 27

Answer Key 45

3 **Practice Test** 63

Answer Key 77

4 **Practice Test** 87

Answer Key 103

Introduction

Congratulations on choosing to take the Series 7! By purchasing this book, you've taken the first step toward becoming a registered General Securities Representative.

This guide provides a detailed overview of the Series 7, so you'll know exactly what to expect on test day. We'll take you through all the concepts covered on the test and give you the opportunity to test your knowledge with practice questions. Even if it's been a while since you last took a major test, don't worry; we'll make sure you're more than ready!

What Is the Series 7?

The Series 7 exam measures a candidate's competency to perform the duties of a General Securities Representative. To become a registered General Securities Representative, a candidate must pass both the Series 7 exam and the Securities Industry Essentials (SIE) exam. The Series 7 is administered by the Financial Industry Regulatory Authority, Inc. (FINRA).

What's on the Series 7?

The candidate must be familiar with the four major functions that make up the exam. The subject matter and percentages of the exam are as follows:

WHAT'S on the Series 7?			
FUNCTION	DESCRIPTION	PERCENTAGE OF EXAM	NUMBER OF QUESTIONS
1	Seeks Business for the Broker-Dealer from Customers and Potential Customers	7%	9

continued on next page

WHAT'S on the Series 7? (continued)			
FUNCTION	**DESCRIPTION**	**PERCENTAGE OF EXAM**	**NUMBER OF QUESTIONS**
2	Opens Accounts after Obtaining and Evaluating Customers' Financial Profile and Investment Objectives	9%	11
3	Provides Customers with Information about Investments, Makes Recommendations, Transfers Assets, and Maintains Appropriate Records	73%	91
4	Obtains and Verifies Customers' Purchase and Sales Instructions and Agreements; Processes, Completes, and Confirms Transactions	11%	14
Total	3 hours and 45 minutes		125 (+10 pretest)

Functions

Function 1, Seeks Business for the Broker-Dealer from Customers and Potential Customers, makes up 7% of the exam, or nine questions. These questions address your ability to communicate with customers, develop promotional materials, appropriately distribute marketing materials, and solicit business when describing investment products and services. Related FINRA rules and US Securities and Exchange Commission (SEC) rules and regulations may be covered.

Function 2, Opens Accounts after Obtaining and Evaluating Customers' Financial Profile and Investment Objectives, makes up 9% of the exam (eleven questions). These questions test your ability to inform customers about different types of accounts; provide disclosures about various account types and restrictions; obtain and update customer information and documentation, including legal documents; identify and address suspicious activity; obtain customer investment profile information, like the customer's other security holdings, tax status, and investment objectives; and obtain supervisory approvals required to open accounts.

The bulk of the test will address Function 3, Provides Customers with Information about Investments, Makes Recommendations, Transfers Assets, and Maintains Appropriate Records. These questions make up 73% of the exam, or ninety-one questions. These questions address discussing investment strategies, risks, and rewards with customers. They also test your ability to communicate market, investment, and research data to customers. Prepare to show that you understand how to determine that your investment recommendations meet applicable standards. Questions will also address required disclosures regarding investment products, communicating about account information, processing requests, and retaining documentation.

Function 4, Obtains and Verifies Customers' Purchase and Sales Instructions and Agreements; Processes, Completes, and Confirms Transactions, makes up 11% of the exam, or fourteen questions. Prepare for questions about providing quotes, processing and confirming customer transactions in line with regulatory requirements, and informing customers of delivery obligations and settlement procedures. Expect questions about resolving errors, discrepancies, and complaints, and addressing margin issues.

How Is the Series 7 Administered?

The Series 7 is a computer-based exam. Examinees have three hours and forty-five minutes to complete the exam. Each exam consists of 135 multiple-choice questions. One hundred and twenty-five questions are scored. Ten are pretest, unscored questions. Each question lists four possible answer choices. Only one answer choice is correct.

About This Guide

This guide will help you master the most important test topics and develop critical test-taking skills. We have built features into our books to prepare you for your exam and increase your score. Along with a detailed summary of the test's format, content, and scoring, we offer an in-depth overview of the content knowledge required to pass the test. Throughout the guide, you'll find sidebars that provide interesting information, highlight key concepts, and review content so that you can solidify your understanding. You can also test your knowledge with sample questions throughout the text as well as practice questions. We're pleased you've chosen Trivium to be a part of your journey!

1 Practice Test 1

1. A customer, in a cash account, purchases 1 DEF 60 put for $2 and sells 1 DEF 70 put at $6 when the price of DEF stock is trading at $65. What is the maximum loss for this position?
   A) $200
   B) $400
   C) $600
   D) $800

2. A customer purchases 1 XYZ 60 call for $5 and 1 XYZ 60 put at $3 when the price of XYZ is trading at $62. What is the maximum loss for this position?
   A) $0
   B) $300
   C) $500
   D) $800

3. Which of the following statements is CORRECT?
   A) An American stock option can be exercised any time before expiration.
   B) The buyer of a call must purchase 100 shares of the underlying security at the strike price.
   C) At expiration, a stock option becomes a market order.
   D) The seller of a put is bearish on the market.

4. A customer bought 1 ABC 30 call for $2. For the customer to break even on this option, the market price of ABC stock must be what?
   A) $23
   B) $28
   C) $30
   D) $32

5. A customer paid $1 for a put contract with a strike price of $25. What is the maximum total profit the customer can earn on a single contract of this option?
   A) $24
   B) $2,400
   C) $2,499
   D) $2,500

6. A customer wrote a 35-strike put on XYZ stock. The total option premium collected was $125. The customer does not currently own any shares of XYZ stock. What is the customer's maximum loss on the option position?
   A) $125
   B) $3,375
   C) $3,500
   D) $3,625

7. What is the intrinsic value of a put with a strike price of $20 if the underlying price of the stock is $18?
   A) $0
   B) $2
   C) $200
   D) $2,000

8. What is the ex-dividend date for cash settlement trades?
   A) 4 business days before the record date
   B) 5 business days before the record date
   C) the same day as the record date
   D) 1 day after the record date

9. Which of the following statements is CORRECT concerning warrants?
   A) Warrants generally provide voting rights.
   B) A warrant is a short-term option on shares of stock.
   C) Warrants do not pay dividends.
   D) Warrants cover 100 shares of the underlying stock.

10. A customer buys 1 ABC 40 call for $7 and sells 1 ABC 50 call at $4 when the price of ABC stock is trading at $43. What is the maximum loss for this position?
    A) $300
    B) $400
    C) $700
    D) $1,000

11. If there is no activity in a client's account, how often must the brokerage firm send a statement to the client?
    A) monthly
    B) quarterly
    C) semiannually
    D) yearly

12. What is the ad valorem tax on a property with an assessed value of $550,000, a current market value of $535,000, and a tax rate of 16 mills?
    A) $8,800
    B) $9,600
    C) $10,400
    D) $12,800

13. A customer of Retirement Investment Advisers, Inc., signs the required documentation to convert his retirement account into a discretionary account. The registered representative responsible for the account purchases 2,000 shares of a mutual fund offered by his firm for $50.00 without asking the customer for approval first. One week later, the registered representative sells the shares for a small profit at $50.45, again without contacting the customer. A month after that, the registered representative buys another 2,000 shares of the same mutual fund for $50.00 without asking the customer for approval. Is the registered representative breaking the law?
    A) No, because he has generated a profit.
    B) No, because the customer submitted paperwork to make the account discretionary.
    C) Yes, because he is churning.
    D) Yes, because he failed to notify the customer of his trades before executing them.

14. A registered representative who has limited trading authorization in a client's account may do which of the following?
    A) deduct a monthly fee for handling the account
    B) buy and sell stocks, bonds, warrants, and mutual funds
    C) transfer securities in and out of the client's account
    D) pay money to a third party

15. In early April, a customer sells 1 GCS Jul 40 call at $4 and buys 1 GCS Oct 40 call for $6. Before expiration, the customer executes closing transactions by covering (repurchasing) the Jul 40 call for $7 per share and selling the Oct 40 call for $8 per share. What is the customer's profit or loss?
    A) $100 profit
    B) $100 loss
    C) $300 profit
    D) $300 loss

16. Firm X is a member of a selling group, and Firm Y is not a participant in the offering. Firm X sells a small number of shares to Firm Y at a price that is slightly below the public offering price. This is considered to be what?

    A) illegal
    B) reallowance
    C) retention
    D) undercutting

17. A customer purchases 1 XYZ 60 call for $5 and 1 XYZ 60 put for $3 when the price of XYZ is trading at $62. If the price of XYZ closes at $75 on the expiration date and the customer exercises the call, what is her profit or loss?

    A) $700 profit
    B) $700 loss
    C) $800 profit
    D) $800 loss

18. A customer purchases 1 XYZ 60 call for $5 and 1 XYZ 60 put for $3 when the price of XYZ is trading at $62. If the price of XYZ moves to $52 upon expiration and the customer exercises the put, what is his profit or loss?

    A) $0
    B) $300 profit
    C) $800 loss
    D) $800 profit

19. According to the Capital Asset Pricing Model, a stock that pays no dividends and has no market risk premium should appreciate at what rate?

    A) 0%
    B) risk-free rate
    C) prime rate
    D) LIBOR

20. A customer sells 1 MNO 40 call at $3 and 1 MNO 40 put at $6 when the price of MNO stock is trading at $34. If the price of MNO moves to $30 upon expiration and the customer receives an exercise notice, what is her profit or loss?

    A) $100 loss
    B) $300 profit
    C) $300 loss
    D) $900 profit

21. A customer sells 1 MNO 40 call at $3 and 1 MNO 40 put at $6 when the price of MNO is trading at $34. What is the maximum gain for this position?

    A) $300
    B) $400
    C) $600
    D) $900

22. The Securities Act of 1933 pertains to which securities market?

    A) primary
    B) secondary
    C) third
    D) fourth

23. A customer with no other securities positions sells 1 ABC Oct 25 put at $2 when the price of ABC stock is $25 per share. If the writer is assigned an exercise notice and sells the ABC stock for $22 per share, what is the resulting profit or loss?

    A) $100 profit
    B) $100 loss
    C) $200 profit
    D) $200 loss

24. A customer with no other securities positions sells 1 ABC Oct 25 put at $2 when the price of ABC stock is $25 per share. What is the maximum loss the writer could sustain just before expiration?

    A) $200
    B) $2,300
    C) $2,500
    D) $2,700

25. A customer with no other securities positions sells 1 ABC Oct 25 put for a premium of $2 when the price of ABC stock is $25 per share. Upon expiration, what is the underlying stock price at which the writer will break even?

    A) $23
    B) $25
    C) $27
    D) $29

26. For a convertible security, what is the conversion ratio?
    A) the ratio of the client's assets to the client's liabilities in a margin account
    B) the ratio of the conversion price of a bond to the interest rate
    C) the ratio of the par value of the convertible bond to the conversion price of the equity
    D) the current price of the common stock to the dividend yield

27. A city issuing bonds would retain the services of what type of attorney to issue a legal opinion?
    A) city attorney
    B) district attorney
    C) trust attorney
    D) bond counsel

28. If someone wants to review the performance of a revenue bond that matures in 30 years, where would that person look?
    A) Bond Buyer 20 Bond Index
    B) Bond Buyer 30 Bond Index
    C) Revenue Bond Index
    D) Visible Supply

29. A customer with no other securities positions sells 1 ABC Sep 30 put for a premium of $3 when the price of ABC stock is $30 per share. What is her maximum profit?
    A) $3
    B) $30
    C) $300
    D) unlimited

30. What is cash flow?
    A) gross income less operating expenses and mortgage costs
    B) gross income less depreciation plus mortgage costs
    C) gross income plus depreciation plus operating expenses
    D) net income less operating expenses, mortgage costs, and depreciation

31. Which of the following would be quoted as 5.10% bid – 5.00% ask?
    A) Treasury bills
    B) Treasury notes
    C) Treasury bonds
    D) Treasury receipts

32. A customer looking to buy a Treasury security directly from the US government that matures in 10 years would choose which of the following?
    A) Treasury bonds
    B) Treasury notes
    C) Treasury bills
    D) Treasury STRIPS

33. What securities are listed in the yellow sheets?
    A) OTC common stocks
    B) OTC corporate bonds
    C) NYSE-listed stocks
    D) municipal bonds

34. A client tells you to buy 340 shares of Company XYZ at $45 per share, with the note "AON." Two hundred shares are bought at $45, but then the price rises to $47. What will happen to the client's order?
    A) He will not be filled with any shares.
    B) He will buy 200 shares at $47 because that is where the stock price is now.
    C) He won't trade with you because you didn't get the order he wanted.
    D) The entire order will be executed at $46 because that is the average price.

35. A DK notice does NOT need to be sent under which of the following circumstances?
    A) when a discrepancy is discovered between the trade and settlement date
    B) when the trade confirmations exchanged between dealers show different securities
    C) when a broker-dealer fails to send a confirmation to the contra broker-dealer
    D) when a broker-dealer sends an erroneous confirmation to a customer

36. When will an owner in a GNMA pool receive a pass-through of interest and principal?
    A) monthly
    B) quarterly
    C) semiannually
    D) annually

37. A customer wants to sell 10 uncovered XYZ Jun 40 calls at $4\frac{3}{4}$ when the underlying stock is trading at $42. What is the customer's maximum gain?
    A) $2,000
    B) $2,750
    C) $3,525
    D) $4,750

38. Under what circumstances is a broker-dealer permitted to charge both a commission and a markup beyond the execution price on a customer trade?
    A) if disclosed to the customer
    B) through the consent of the customer
    C) with the permission of the exchange or the FINRA
    D) under no circumstances

39. General Mfg. is offering new shares to the public through a rights offering. The existing shares are trading at $30.00 per share (ex-rights), and the offering has a subscription price of $29.00 per share. The corporation is offering 200,000 new shares and has one million shares already outstanding. What is the value of the right?
    A) $0.20
    B) $0.25
    C) $0.40
    D) $0.50

40. Which of the following describes what the OTC market consists of?
    A) trades in securities listed on exchanges
    B) anyone making an offer or bid in the market
    C) institutional investors who deal directly with other institutional investors
    D) broker-dealers who negotiate securities trades not listed on an exchange

41. What is the formula for a short margin account?
    A) credit balance minus short market value equals equity
    B) credit balance plus equity equals short market value
    C) short market value minus credit balance equals equity
    D) credit balance plus short market value equals equity

42. Which of the following guarantees are provided in a variable annuity?
    A) fixed number of dollar payments each month for the life of the annuitant
    B) lifetime income that is based on a fluctuating value of a fixed number of units each month
    C) payments of a fixed number of dollars each month for a predetermined term of years
    D) payments based on a fixed value of a fluctuating number of accumulation units each month

43. ACME Electronics has a 7% cumulative and simple preferred stock outstanding. The company did not pay any dividends last year, marking the first interruption to its dividend program in a decade. Later this year, the company will resume its dividend for common stock. How much in dividends will the company pay this year to a preferred stockholder whose holdings have a par value of $100,000?
    A) $0
    B) $7,000 per share
    C) $14,000 per share
    D) $14,490 per share

44. A registered representative wants to send a letter to a potential customer regarding a security recommended in a telephone conversation. Whose permission must the registered representative receive?
    A) NYSE
    B) SEC
    C) branch office manager
    D) no prior approval is required

45. Which of the following can be described as the third market?
    A) direct trades between individual investors
    B) trades in listed securities that occur on the NYSE
    C) direct trades between institutional investors
    D) trades in listed securities that occur OTC

46. Which of the following BEST characterizes REITs?
    A) They are investment vehicles that offer diversification.
    B) Because REITs are trusts, they are not required to operate under the same rules as other public companies
    C) They are only required to have fifty shareholders at a minimum.
    D) They are typically traded through Series A investments.

47. A UIT is characterized by which of the following?
    A) a managed portfolio of only Treasury bills and Treasury notes
    B) an unmanaged portfolio of stocks and bonds
    C) a managed portfolio of ETFs
    D) a portfolio designed to provide a basket of options so the investor can write calls when he wishes

48. Radio Mast Corp. is an REIT. This year, the corporation earned taxable income of $20 million, and it has five million shares outstanding. It declares a dividend in December to be paid in January of next year. What is the minimum amount of the per-share dividend?
    A) $4.00
    B) $3.80
    C) $3.60
    D) $3.40

49. The sequence of disclosures in a real estate limited partnership offering is governed under what guidance?
    A) Securities Act Industry Guide 4
    B) Securities Act Industry Guide 5
    C) Securities Act Industry Guide 6
    D) Securities Act Industry Guide 7

50. The state of Michigan issues bonds to be used to build a toll bridge. The issue will be considered moral obligation bonds. The resulting bridge fails to generate adequate revenue to make the stipulated principal and interest payments to the bondholders. What action may be taken on behalf of the bondholders to receive their payments?
    A) special assessment by the municipality
    B) administrative actions
    C) judicial action by the bondholders
    D) legislative apportionment

51. What is the time value of a $50-strike call that is worth $4 when the market price of its underlying stock is $52?
    A) $2
    B) $4
    C) $6
    D) $8

52. Under Regulation SHO, what is the term for equity securities that have an aggregate fail to deliver position at a registered clearing agency of 10,000 shares or more, and that equal or exceed 0.5% of the total shares outstanding for five consecutive settlement days or more?
    A) block trade
    B) threshold security
    C) hard-to-borrow stocks
    D) naked short sale

53. Which of the following is permitted under Regulation SHO to sell shares of stock without first owning them, borrowing them, or knowing where to find them?
    A) retail customer
    B) program trader
    C) bona fide market maker
    D) Under no circumstances is this permitted.

54. What is the minimum equity requirement under Regulation T when a customer sells 100 shares of stock QRS short at $10 per share in an account containing no other positions?
    A) 30% of market value
    B) 100% of market value
    C) 150% of market value
    D) 200% of market value

55. Fluctuations of the value of an annuity unit of a variable annuity contract will correspond most closely with fluctuations in what?
    A) inflation
    B) Standard & Poor's index
    C) the value of securities held in the separate account
    D) Dow Jones Industrial Average index

56. An investor who redeems mutual fund shares receives a payment that is based on
    A) POP on the day the redemption request is received.
    B) NAV on the day the redemption request is received.
    C) NAV on the day the redemption request is processed.
    D) mid-price on the day the redemption request is processed.

57. Which type of bond is issued by a railroad and collateralized by railroad cars?
    A) revenue bond
    B) mortgage bond
    C) equipment trust certificate
    D) special situation bond

58. XYZ Securities is owned by General Conglomerate Corp. (GCC). A registered representative of XYZ Securities sells 100 shares of GCC to a public customer. What is this considered to be?
    A) a violation of FINRA Conduct Rules
    B) a control relationship that must be disclosed to the customer
    C) permissible if the customer gives written permission before the order is placed
    D) no special considerations required in this circumstance

59. NASDAQ Level I access is characterized by which of the following?
    A) shows market depth
    B) shows how many shares the market maker wants
    C) is the best way to execute a trade
    D) gives real-time best bid/offer quotes only

60. A customer enters an order to purchase stock at $15.00 per share. The trade report that states that the stock was bought at $14.50 is given to the registered representative and then relayed to the customer. The next day, it is discovered that the trade was actually executed at $15.00 per share. What price must be paid for the stock and by whom?
    A) The firm must sell the stock to the customer at $14.50 due to the error.
    B) The registered representative must absorb the loss and pay $15.00 for the stock.
    C) The customer must pay $15.00 per share for the stock.
    D) The exchange that executed the trade will absorb the loss in its escrow account, upon application by the firm.

61. A corporate bond
    A) is issued by the government strictly to corporations.
    B) is lower risk than a government bond because only AAA-rated companies can issue corporate bonds.
    C) can be used by the market maker to guarantee a profit on an investment for a client.
    D) is issued by any corporation and sold to investors, usually with a higher interest rate than government bonds.

62. Which of the following constitutes a good delivery?
    A) delivery of a 525-share certificate for a transaction of 525 shares
    B) delivery of four 50-share certificates for a transaction of 200 shares
    C) bonds that are mutilated
    D) bonds with a coupon that had been canceled due to a bona fide error

63. How long is Form 144 effective?
    A) 30 days
    B) 60 days
    C) 90 days
    D) when the securities are sold

64. Company ABC has four million shares of treasury stock. Which of the following is a characteristic of this type of stock?
    A) These shares pay dividends to every investor who holds them, provided the investor has over $250,000 in investable assets.
    B) These shares have voting rights for preferred investors.
    C) These shares are included when calculating shares outstanding.
    D) These shares could have come from a repurchase or buyback, or they may have never been issued to the public.

65. What is the common stock of an automobile maker considered?
    A) emerging growth
    B) cyclical
    C) defensive
    D) special situation

66. A customer wants to withdraw her vested interest in a corporate retirement plan by lump sum and put the money in an IRA. Under the rules for IRA rollovers, when would the proceeds need to be rolled over into the IRA before incurring a tax penalty?
    A) 30 days
    B) 60 days
    C) 90 days
    D) 1 year

67. If the bid price of an open-end fund is $15 per share and the ask price is $16 per share, what is the fund's sales charge (SC) percentage?
    A) 6.00%
    B) 6.25%
    C) 8.00%
    D) 8.50%

68. A customer purchases a 9.0% corporate bond for $92 with a maturity of 20 years. What is the approximate yield to maturity?
    A) 8.9%
    B) 9.8%
    C) 10.1%
    D) 10.3%

69. A securities firm acting as consultant to ACME Mfg. Corp. has received a copy of a list with the company's shareholders. What is the firm permitted to do with this information?
    A) The firm may use this list for prospecting new customers at its own discretion.
    B) The firm may use this list for prospecting only with ACME Mfg. Corp.'s written permission.
    C) The firm is not permitted to use the list.
    D) The firm is permitted to rent this list to other disinterested parties.

70. A registered representative inputs a customer's data for a variable annuity program on the computer to show the hypothetical results over a contract's life on a computer screen. According to FINRA rules, what rate of return assumptions must the screen result use?
    A) A 0% and a maximum rate of 12% must be used; any rate between 0% and 12% may be used.
    B) A 0% rate must be used, and any other rates up to a maximum of 12% may be used, provided the largest rate used is reasonable in relation to the market and available investment options.
    C) Rates of return would not be dictated by the FINRA for the personalized screen presentation.
    D) A 0% rate must be used, but any other rates may be used as long as the maximum rate is a reasonable expectation of market conditions and investment options available.

71. *ADR* stands for which of the following?
    A) American depositary receipt: shares of a foreign stock issued by a US bank, traded on a US exchange
    B) America's debenture request: an order to buy debentures during World War II to help boost the US economy
    C) American depositary receipt: shares of a US stock, issued by a US bank, traded on a foreign exchange
    D) American depositary request: shares of a foreign stock, issued by a foreign bank, traded only on the NASDAQ

72. The best price for a security is $25 per share, which is offered by a market maker. Firm XYZ has a customer order to buy the security. Firm XYZ calls Firm ABC and asks that firm to sell the security. Firm ABC buys the security from the market maker and sells it to Firm XYZ, who in turn sells the security to the customer. Both Firm ABC and Firm XYZ charge commissions on this transaction. What is this an example of?
  A) hypothecation
  B) interpositioning
  C) backing away
  D) front-running

73. If a city that has sold revenue bonds to finance the construction of a toll bridge experiences a collapse of the bridge during construction, what call provision would the city invoke?
  A) catastrophe call
  B) defeasance call
  C) sinking fund call
  D) disaster call

74. If the initial transaction in a margin account is the purchase of 100 shares of a security at $16 per share, what is the NYSE minimum margin?
  A) $800
  B) $1,000
  C) $1,600
  D) $2,000

75. The goals of limited partnerships under the Tax Reform Act of 1986 emphasize which of the following?
  A) tax shelter
  B) income
  C) depreciation
  D) tax credits

76. DEF Corp. is listed on the NYSE. XYZ Securities sells 100 shares of DEF to a customer from its own account. If this trade is not executed on the floor of an exchange, it must be reported
  A) within 90 seconds of the trade taking place.
  B) on the day of the trade (T + 0).
  C) within 5 business days after the trade takes place (T + 5).
  D) within 7 business days after the trade takes place (T + 7).

77. When is payment for the regular-way purchase of a round lot of US Treasury notes and bonds due?
  A) trade day
  B) following business day
  C) the fifth business day after the trade date
  D) the seventh business day after the trade date

78. Who has the primary enforcement responsibility of MSRB regulations over a company that decides to form a subsidiary to sell municipal bonds?
  A) FINRA
  B) SIPC
  C) NYSE
  D) MSRB

79. The term *underwriting* is used in conjunction with what?
  A) firms participating in the distribution of a new security issue
  B) firms participating in the distribution of a secondary issue
  C) firms acting as a broker in the secondary market
  D) firms acting as a dealer in the secondary market

80. Which of the following is required to register as an investment adviser?
  A) broker-dealers
  B) banks
  C) a publisher of an investment newsletter
  D) a general circulation newspaper

81. When do PM-settled listed options that are expiring cease trading?
  A) at 2 p.m. central time; 3 p.m. eastern time on the business day before expiration date
  B) at 2 p.m. central time; 3 p.m. eastern time on the expiration date
  C) at 3 p.m. central time; 4 p.m. eastern time on the business day before expiration date
  D) at 3 p.m. central time; 4 p.m. eastern time on the expiration date

82. Which of the following BEST characterizes program trading?
    A) It is only available to small investors.
    B) It is not allowed by the NYSE.
    C) It is used for money management.
    D) It is known as computer-aided trading.

83. Three firms are participating in the underwriting of a bond issued by a municipality. A customer wants to purchase one of these bonds but first wants to review the official statement. In which case would Securities Firm A NOT have to give an official statement to the customer?
    A) Securities Firm A is the managing underwriter.
    B) The customer is deemed a sophisticated investor.
    C) The municipality uses a competitive bid process to form the underwriting syndicate.
    D) The municipality has not yet made an official statement available.

84. A municipal securities representative receives an order from a customer that the representative believes is not suitable and advises the customer as much, but the customer insists on the trade. What should the representative do?
    A) execute the order after obtaining approval of the firm's municipal securities principal
    B) execute the order with approval from the MSRB
    C) not execute the order
    D) execute the order anyway

85. A trader at an investment bank gives a customer an indicative bid of $45.01 for 10,000 shares of TUV stock over the phone. The customer promptly and clearly responds with a limit order to sell 10,000 shares at that price. At the closing bell, TUV stock is trading below $45.00 and the order remains unfilled. Regulators would consider the trader's act to be what?
    A) backing away
    B) front-running
    C) spoofing
    D) lawful

86. A municipal security may NOT be purchased from which party in the secondary market?
    A) a broker's brokers
    B) dealers
    C) issuers
    D) customers

87. Which of the following municipal bonds would have the greatest increase in price when interest rates fall?
    A) discount bond maturing in 1 year
    B) premium bond maturing in 1 year
    C) discount bond maturing in 20 years
    D) premium bond maturing in 20 years

88. Of the following, who may NOT trade for their own account?
    A) a registered options trader
    B) a floor broker
    C) a market maker
    D) a competitive options trader

89. Which of the following purchases has the LOWEST degree of risk to capital?
    A) common stocks
    B) options
    C) corporate bonds
    D) warrants

90. How long is the settlement period for a new issue of a municipal bond?
    A) 5 business days (T + 5)
    B) 7 business days (T + 7)
    C) 30 calendar days
    D) cannot be determined

91. What is a municipal securities firm required to do when receiving an order from a customer?
    A) make a reasonable effort to obtain a fair and reasonable price
    B) contact at least three market makers in the issue
    C) execute the order at exactly its fair market value
    D) obtain a fair and reasonable price

92. Which of the following is addressed by Regulation ATS?
   A) dark pools
   B) short selling
   C) trading halts
   D) research reports

93. What type of order does a customer enter to sell 100 shares of common stock at $25 per share?
   A) a market order
   B) a limit order
   C) a stop order
   D) a stop-limit order

94. A customer purchased a Mar 30 put on ABC stock and a Mar 30 call on ABC stock. What is this position called?
   A) long straddle
   B) vertical spread
   C) short straddle
   D) option spread

95. Which of the following statements is NOT correct regarding municipal securities trading in the secondary market?
   A) Municipal securities trade OTC.
   B) Municipal securities may be listed on the NASDAQ.
   C) The largest participants are institutional investors.
   D) Most trades are performed on a dealer basis.

96. What is the maximum duration for LEAPS?
   A) 3 months
   B) 6 months
   C) 12 months
   D) more than 36 months

97. A FINRA-member firm is required to maintain records of written customer complaints for at LEAST how long?
   A) 6 months
   B) 1 year
   C) 2 years
   D) 4 years

98. How is a limit order typically characterized?
   A) It is a buy or sell order at a specific price or better.
   B) It can only be executed if the client has over $2 million in investable assets.
   C) It is guaranteed to execute before the market closes.
   D) It enables the client to fill her order as soon as the market opens.

99. On what date do monthly equity options expire?
   A) the last Friday of the expiration month at 2 p.m.
   B) the third Friday of the expiration month at 2 p.m.
   C) the Saturday following the last Friday of the expiration month
   D) the Saturday following the third Friday of the expiration month

100. Which of the following activities is permissible under the Securities Act of 1933?
   A) borrowing shares and selling them to a person making a tender offer for the shares
   B) making a stabilizing bid that does not involve a new issue
   C) a firm hypothecating a customer's securities to a bank to finance the debit balance
   D) a firm loaning a customer money to purchase a new issue

101. The president of an exchange-listed company that has four million shares outstanding files a notice of sale and wants to sell as many shares as possible in the next 90 days. The weekly volume for the stock recently was (for the weeks' endings): 25,000 shares (Feb 3); 30,000 shares (Feb 10); 40,000 shares (Feb 17); 35,000 shares (Feb 24); 30,000 shares (today, Mar 1). At most, how many shares may the company president sell?
   A) 32,000 shares
   B) 32,500 shares
   C) 33,750 shares
   D) 40,000 shares

102. Rule 144 pertains to which of the following?
    A) public resale of restricted and control securities
    B) the amount of time an option must be held before a C-level executive can sell it (144 days)
    C) the amount of time needed before a corporation can send a red herring to potential investors
    D) the maximum number of securities a client is allowed to keep in one account

103. A market-on-close order placed at noon to sell 1,000 shares of ABC stock on the NYSE executes when?
    A) as close to the market as possible
    B) at the closing price of the day
    C) at the bid price immediately before the close
    D) at the ask price immediately before the close

104. What is one purpose of a redemption notice?
    A) issue stock
    B) liquidate a mutual fund
    C) call a bond issue
    D) provide a statement of intent to issue debt

105. A stop-loss order is characterized by which of the following?
    A) It guarantees complete execution before too much of the investor's money is lost.
    B) It is also known as a "stop order" or "stop-market order."
    C) It can only be executed before 10:30 a.m. central time because all orders must go through Chicago.
    D) It should never be accepted by the broker because it puts the firm at too much risk.

106. The FINRA 5% markup policy is regulatory guidance that applies to a member who acts as
    A) agent.
    B) principal.
    C) both agent and principal.
    D) neither agent nor principal.

107. Which of the following is EXCLUDED from the definition of sales literature under the FINRA Rules of Fair Practice?
    A) research reports
    B) reprints or excerpts from other advertisements
    C) market letters
    D) tombstone ads

108. A registered representative sold 100 shares of ABC, a new stock issue, to a customer at the offering price of $25 per share. A month later, ABC is offered in the market at $22. If the customer expresses strong concern about the decline in value, which statement is CORRECT regarding the representative's offer to buy 100 shares from the customer for $24 per share?
    A) It would not violate FINRA rules because the customer bears a third of the loss.
    B) It would violate FINRA rules against guaranteeing a customer against loss.
    C) It would not violate FINRA rules because ABC was a new issue.
    D) This is a violation of FINRA rules against stabilizing quotes on a new issue.

109. In October, a customer buys 1 XYZ Jan 30 put for $4 and sells 1 XYZ Jan 40 put at $13. At which of the following prices of the underlying stock would the long option leg be in-the-money?
    A) $41
    B) $30
    C) $32
    D) $25

110. Which of the following statements applies to an investment bank that has agreed to a firm commitment underwriting?
    A) The investment bank must purchase shares that remain unsold after the standby period, at the subscription price.
    B) The investment bank must purchase all of the securities from the issuer.
    C) The investment bank is not obligated to purchase any securities from the issuer.
    D) This type of offering is not desirable for the issuer, because the issuer loses the flexibility to allocate shares as needed.

111. A straddle writer anticipates which of the following?
    A) a stock price decrease
    B) a stock price increase
    C) no significant movement in the price of the stock in either direction
    D) a substantial movement in the price of the stock either up or down

112. What is the intrinsic value of an option?
    A) the amount of premium that exceeds the option's in-the-money value
    B) the amount a customer must pay at the close
    C) the amount that the option is in-the-money
    D) the maximum profit

113. Which of the following BEST describes an oil and gas direct participation program exploratory well?
    A) one that has been drilled in an unproven field and is located away from proven fields
    B) one that has been drilled in proximity to oil-producing wells
    C) a well with a lower return to investors than development wells
    D) one that receives large investment tax credits

114. A company first sold stock publicly in 1972. In 1977, it repurchased 200,000 shares. Today, it is selling 500,000 shares to the public, 200,000 of which were repurchased in 1977. This is BEST described as what?
    A) initial offering
    B) primary offering
    C) split offering
    D) secondary offering

115. Which of the following is NOT an activity of an investment banker?
    A) accept time and demand deposits
    B) act as underwriter
    C) purchase securities for its own account
    D) participate in the distribution of new issues

116. The long holder of a listed call option on PQR stock exercises the contract in order to buy 100 shares for the contract's strike price. What is the settlement time for this exercise transaction?
    A) T + 0
    B) T + 1
    C) T + 2
    D) T + 3

117. An order to buy 400 shares of ABC at $35, immediate-or-cancel, is entered before the market opening. The following trades occur in ABC when trading begins: 100 shares at $35; 200 shares at $35; and 100 shares at $35. How many shares did this order receive?
    A) 100
    B) 200
    C) 300
    D) 400

118. What is the purpose of a tombstone ad?
    A) redeem a stock issue
    B) call a mutual fund
    C) call a bond issue
    D) provide a statement of fact

119. A customer places an order on the NYSE at 3:30 p.m. EST to buy 100 shares of XYZ stock market-on-close. At what price would this order be executed?
    A) the bid price immediately before the closing bell
    B) the price of the closing auction
    C) the offer price immediately after the closing bell
    D) the next day's opening price because the order was placed after 3:00 p.m.

120. The specialist for XYZ stock has a good-till-canceled order on the books to purchase ten shares for $40.00 per share. The next morning, XYZ stock starts trading without a $0.55 dividend. What is the limit order on the book?
    A) $39.45
    B) $39.63
    C) $39.50
    D) $39.38

121. When may a broker buy securities in a customer's account without authorization?
    A) when the broker promptly notifies the client in writing after the securities have been purchased
    B) when the broker advises a branch office manager that the securities will be purchased
    C) when the client is unavailable to buy the securities himself
    D) when the customer has given the representative discretion as to time and price earlier in the day

122. A customer buys 100 shares of ADM for $30 and sells 1 ADM Oct 30 call at $8. What is the breakeven for this position?
    A) $22
    B) $24
    C) $30
    D) $38

123. A customer is long 1 Apr 40 call. On ex-date of a 2-for-1 stock split, the customer will be long
    A) 1 Apr 40 call for 100 shares.
    B) 1 Apr 20 call for 200 shares.
    C) 2 Apr 20 calls for 100 shares each.
    D) 2 Apr 40 calls for 100 shares each.

124. Which of the following corporate characteristics is the MOST difficult for a limited partnership to avoid?
    A) perpetuity
    B) limited liability
    C) centralized management
    D) free transferability of interests

125. A nonaffiliated person purchases and fully pays for restricted Acme Corp. stock today. Acme Corp. is subject to the reporting requirements of the Securities Exchange Act of 1934. When may this stock be sold?
    A) 6 months from today
    B) 12 months from today
    C) 2 years from today
    D) Nonaffiliated persons are not subject to holding periods.

126. In technical analysis, a consolidating market has what type of trend line?
    A) exponential
    B) sideways
    C) upward
    D) downward

127. In a NYSE Bond quote yield column, what does the notation *ZR* mean?
    A) convertible bond
    B) deep discount
    C) yield not available
    D) zero coupon

128. If a customer enters an order to buy 10,000 shares of XYZ for $25 and tells her broker that she will not accept a partial fill, what is this known as?
    A) immediate-or-cancel
    B) fill-or-kill
    C) all or none
    D) not held

129. A company's stock closed today at $30.00 per share, with the stock trading ex-dividend tomorrow. The upcoming dividend is $0.70 per share. Neglecting interest rates, which of the following American-style call options expiring next week is MOST likely to be exercised early? (Closing bid and ask prices from the option chain are shown.)
    A) 31 call ($0.60 bid, $0.65 ask)
    B) 30 call ($1.20 bid, $1.25 ask)
    C) 29 call ($1.80 bid, $1.90 ask)
    D) 28 call ($2.40 bid, $2.60 ask)

130. Why is arbitration preferred over litigation to settle disputes in the securities industry?
    A) It is often less costly than litigation.
    B) It results in decisions that are more binding than those of local courts.
    C) It excludes those arguments from personnel of firms outside the industry.
    D) It allows the parties more opportunity to present their cases.

131. Which of the following types of option transactions are considered the MOST speculative?
- **A)** selling a spread position
- **B)** writing an uncovered call
- **C)** holding a call
- **D)** holding a spread position

132. In June, a customer sells 1 DEF Sep 40 put at $5 and sells 1 DEF Sep 40 call at $3 when the price of DEF is trading at $38. At expiration, the put is assigned, and the resulting shares are sold at $35. The call expires unexercised. What is the profit or loss on this transaction?
- **A)** $300 profit
- **B)** $500 profit
- **C)** $500 loss
- **D)** $800 loss

133. Where do the deductions primarily come from in the first year of an oil and gas drilling partnership?
- **A)** depreciation
- **B)** depletion
- **C)** intangible drilling costs
- **D)** investment tax credits

134. What BEST describes the cooling-off period?
- **A)** the time between the registration filing and the effective date
- **B)** the date the offering is released by the SEC
- **C)** the period before the filing of the registration statement
- **D)** the period before any errors in the prospectus are corrected

135. A customer has a balance in an account that can be withdrawn immediately upon request. How often should statements be sent to the customer?
- **A)** monthly
- **B)** quarterly
- **C)** semiannually
- **D)** annually

Answer Key

1. **C)** This strategy is a bull put spread; it is used when the investor expects the price of the asset to increase. For a vertical credit spread (like a bull put spread or a bear call spread), find the difference between the strike prices minus the net credit (premium collected up front) to determine the maximum loss. Here, the difference between the strike prices is $10 (70 - 60 = 10), and the net credit is $4 ($6 - $2 = $4). $10 - $4 = $6. Use the 100 multiplier to find the maximum loss: $6 × 100 = $600.

2. **D)** This strategy of buying 1 call and 1 put on the same strike is called a straddle. The maximum loss for calls and the maximum loss for puts is the premium paid. Use the 100 multiplier to determine that the customer paid $500 ($5 × 100) for 1 XYZ call and $300 ($3 × 100) for 1 XYZ put. The maximum loss is the combined cost paid by the customer: $500 + $300 = $800.

3. **A)** American-style options can be exercised at any time on or before the expiration date. A call holder (buyer) has the right to buy the underlying security at the strike price but is not obligated to do so. When an option expires, it becomes worthless. Puts protect against declines in the price of the underlying stock and can be thought of as a form of insurance for holders of that stock. The writer (seller) of a put seeks to profit from the premium paid for that insurance.

4. **D)** To break even, the option's intrinsic value must equal the premium paid for the option. The breakeven for a call (regardless of whether it is bought or sold) is the strike price plus the premium paid. Since the strike price for the call is $30 and the premium paid is $2, the customer breaks even when the price of the underlying stock is $32 ($30 + $2 = $32).

5. **B)** The maximum profit for the holder of a put is the strike price less the premium paid. Being long a put contract gives the holder the right to sell 100 shares of stock at the strike price in a falling (bearish) market. If the underlying market price were to fall to $0, the holder could exercise the put and sell 100 shares of stock for $2,500 (1 contract = 100 shares), resulting in a profit of $2,400 ($2,500 - $100 premium paid = $2,400).

6. **B)** The maximum potential loss for a put writer (or put seller) is the strike price less the premium received. Since it is a bullish strategy, if the market price of XYZ stock goes to $0, the writer will have to buy 100 shares of stock from the long holder of the put at $35 per share ($3,500). But because the writer received a premium of $1.25 ($125 total) up front, her maximum loss would be $3,500 - $125 = $3,375.

7. **B)** The intrinsic value for a put is the strike price minus the spot price, floored at zero. To calculate the intrinsic value of a put option, subtract the stock price ($18) from the strike price ($20). The market price is $18, which is below the strike price of $20: $20 - $18 = $2. Intrinsic value can never be negative, so put options with a strike price below the price of the underlying stock have zero intrinsic value.

8. **D)** The ex-dividend date for trades settled in cash is the business day following the record date.

9. **C)** A warrant gives a customer the right to buy a stock on (or sometimes before) a specific date at a specific price. Warrants are not stocks, and they do not pay dividends or entitle the holder to vote in shareholder meetings. Warrants also differ from listed options in several ways. They can be short or long term, may cover more or less than 100 shares, and are not backed by

the Options Clearing Corp. (OCC). An option exercise involves the purchase or exchange of previously issued market shares of the underlying security, but shares used to settle a warrant exercise dilute the equity of the company.

10. **A)** This position is a bull call spread. The call with the lower strike price is purchased, and the call with the higher strike price is sold, creating a net debit of $3 ($7 − $4 = $3). Using the 100 multiplier, a $300 total premium outlay is found ($3 × 100 = $300). The debit is the maximum loss because the long put covers the risk of the short put.

11. **B)** If there is no activity in the account, the client receives quarterly statements. If there is activity, the client receives a monthly statement.

12. **A)** The assessed value, rather than the current market value, is used when calculating taxes. It is important to know that a mill is equal to 0.001 (one-thousandth of $1) when performing the calculation. Therefore, the taxes are calculated by multiplying the assessed value of the property ($550,000) by 16 by a mill ($550,000 × 16 × 0.001 = $8,800).

13. **C)** A registered representative is permitted to make trades in a discretionary account without the prior knowledge or instructions of the customer. However, this situation is an example of churning, an unlawful practice whereby a registered representative makes unnecessary trades in a customer account to generate commissions or sales charges (SCs). While churning is sometimes difficult to prove, a rapid series of buys and sells in a discretionary account intended for long-term investment is a clear red flag. These trades may not be profitable after redemption fees are applied, and even if they are, profits may receive inferior tax treatment depending on the context and circumstances of the client's finances.

14. **B)** Limited trading authorizations allow the registered representative to buy and sell for the client. The registered representative cannot withdraw money or securities.

15. **B)** The customer opened the strategy for a net debit of $2 ($6 − $4 = $2) and closed the strategy for a net credit of $1 ($8 − $7 = $1). The resulting loss is $100 because of the 100 multiplier for listed contracts ($100 × $1 = $100).

16. **B)** Selling a small amount of an offering at a discount to a firm that is not a participant in the selling group is considered a reallowance. It is an incentive for Firm Y to sell shares to its customers.

17. **A)** This position is a long straddle. The buyer of a straddle typically anticipates volatility but is uncertain of which way the market will move. In this case, the stock moves to the upside, so the put option expires worthless but the call option expires with an intrinsic value of $15. The customer makes $1,500 from the in-the-money call but pays $800 for the straddle ($5 + $3 = $8; using the 100 multiplier, $8 × 100 = $800), resulting in a net gain of $700 ($1,500 − $800 = $700).

18. **A)** The stock's price moved to $52, resulting in the long straddle reaching its downside break-even point. The combined premium paid for the straddle was $800 ($5 + $3 = $8; using the 100 multiplier, $8 × 100 = $800), and the intrinsic value of the put upon expiration was also $800. The two cancel out, and the customer's profit or loss is $0.

19. **B)** The Capital Asset Pricing Model (CAPM) describes the expected return as being equal to the risk-free rate plus the product of the investment's beta and its market risk premium. When the risk premium is zero, the expected return equals the risk-free rate. This theoretical rate is typically considered to be greater than zero and is not necessarily equivalent to the prime rate or the London Interbank Offered Rate (LIBOR).

20. **A)** The position is a short straddle. If the market goes neither up nor down, the writer will profit by earning the premiums. Because the price of MNO fell to $30, the put holder (who is now 10 points in-the-money) will exercise her contract, obligating the writer to purchase stock for $40 per share ($4,000). The market value of MNO stock is $30 per share ($3,000), resulting in a loss of $1,000 ($4,000 − $3,000 = $1,000).

Premiums of $9 ($3 + $6 = $9) were received through the sale of the straddle. Use the 100 multiplier: $9 × 100 = $900 total. The net loss would be $100 ($1,000 - $900 = $100), and the call would expire worthless.

21. **D)** This position is a short straddle. The maximum gain on a short straddle is the combined premium received from the sale of the call and the put. Using the 100 multiplier for listed contracts, $3 × 100 = $300 and $6 × 100 = $600. In this example, $300 was received from selling the call, and $600 was received for selling the put for a total maximum profit of $900 ($300 + $600 = $900). To achieve this profit, both the call and the put must expire without being exercised.

22. **A)** The Securities Act of 1933 governs the initial registration and distribution of securities, which is the primary market.

23. **B)** The writer received $2 per share in premium but lost $3 per share on the difference between the $22 and the $25, resulting in a loss of $100.

24. **B)** The put writer must buy the stock for the strike price of $25 if the equity value goes to zero and the option is exercised. Using the 100 multiplier, he would lose $2,500 ($25 × 100 = $2,500) minus the $200 received as a premium ($2 × 100 = $200), or $2,300 in net loss per contract: $2,500 - $200 = $2,300.

25. **A)** $25 - $2 premium received = $23. The contract is in-the-money by the same amount as the initial premium.

26. **C)** The conversion ratio determines the number of shares of common stock for which the convertible bond can be exchanged and is represented as the par value of the convertible bond divided by the conversion price of the equity.

27. **D)** A bond counsel provides legal opinion on the issuance of bonds.

28. **C)** The Revenue Bond Index is composed of 25 revenue bonds with a maturity in 30 years, with a Moody's rating of A1 and an S&P rating of A+. Option A is incorrect, as the 20 Bond Index is an index of general obligation (GO) bonds. Option B is incorrect as there is no 30 Bond Index. Option D is a measurement of the supply of municipal bonds about to be issued within 30 days.

29. **C)** The maximum gain for a short option is the premium received. Use the 100 multiplier: $3 × 100 = $300.

30. **A)** Cash flow is based on the operating expenses and mortgage costs of the program as deducted from gross income.

31. **A)** Treasury bills are quoted and shown in terms of discount from par, whereas other government securities are quoted as a percentage of par in decimal points representing 1/32 of a percent.

32. **B)** Treasury notes have a maturity of 10 years. Separate Trading of Registered Interest and Principal of Securities (STRIPS) must be purchased through a financial institution or brokerage firm.

33. **B)** The yellow sheets provide information about the market makers and their quotes for corporate bonds that are traded over the counter (OTC).

34. **A)** All or none (AON) is a condition in which the broker must fill the order in its entirety or not at all. Here, there is insufficient supply to meet the quantity requested by the client, so the order will be canceled at the close of the market.

35. **D)** Don't know (DK) notices are used when a discrepancy occurs between broker-dealers. They do not involve customers.

36. **A)** The interest and principal payments for Government National Mortgage Association (GNMA) bonds are distributed monthly.

37. **D)** The maximum gain for selling a call is the premium received. Use the 100 multiplier to find the gain:
$4\frac{3}{4} \times 100 = 475$
$475 \times 10 = \$4,750$

38. **D)** A firm may not act as both principal and agent in the same transaction. It can charge a commission or a markup, but not both.

39. **A)** To determine the value, first calculate the number of rights needed to equal one share of common stock, which would be one million outstanding divided by 200,000 new shares: 1,000,000 ÷ 200,000 = 5.

    Next, take the difference between the ex-right market value and the subscription price and divide it by 5:
    $$\frac{(\$30.00 - \$29.00)}{5}$$
    $$= \$\frac{1}{5}$$
    $$= \$0.20$$

40. **D)** The over-the-counter (OTC) market is a negotiated market between broker-dealers.

41. **A)** Credit balance (CB) minus short market value (SMV) equals equity (EQ) in a short margin account: CB − SMV = EQ.

42. **B)** Options A, C, and D describe the guarantees and characteristics of a fixed annuity, not a variable annuity.

43. **C)** Because the preferred stock issue is cumulative, all of its prior-year dividends must be paid before any dividend can be paid to common stockholders. The accumulated dividends do not compound because the preferred stock is simple (noncompounding). Find 7% of $100,000: 0.07 × $100,000 = $7,000. The preferred stockholder will receive a $7,000 payment for this year's dividend and a $7,000 accrual for last year's dividend, for a combined total of $14,000 ($7,000 + $7,000 = $14,000).

44. **C)** Correspondence prepared by a registered representative must be approved by a branch manager of the firm before distribution.

45. **D)** Trades in the third market are usually block trades of stocks listed over the counter (OTC).

46. **A)** Real estate investment trusts (REITs) offer diversification and are required to operate under the same rules as public companies. REITs must have a minimum of one hundred shareholders, and they are traded on major stock exchanges.

47. **B)** A unit investment trust (UIT) is an unmanaged portfolio of stocks and bonds designed to provide capital appreciation and/or dividend income.

48. **C)** Real estate investment trusts (REITs) must distribute 90% or more of their taxable income to shareholders as dividends. They must also invest three-fourths or more of their assets in real estate and derive three-fourths or more of their gross income from real estate–related sources.

49. **B)** The sequence of disclosure for a real estate limited partnership offering is found in Securities Act Industry Guide 5, "Preparation of registration statements relating to interests in real estate limited partnerships." Guide 4 relates to oil and gas; Guide 6 relates to property-casualty insurance; Guide 7 relates to mining.

50. **D)** If a locality defaults on its obligation to repay a moral obligation bond (not backed by the taxing authority or revenues of the issuer), the state's legislature must make a special apportionment to back the principal and interest payments to bondholders. Moral obligation bonds do not carry a legal requirement to avoid default. The government's pledge to pay a moral obligation bond is its backing.

51. **A)** A call option goes in-the-money when the underlying price exceeds the strike price. The difference between the two prices is intrinsic value; the amount of premium that exceeds intrinsic value is known as the time value. An underlying price of $52 and a strike price of $50 mean that the option has $2 of intrinsic value. Since the premium is $4, subtracting the intrinsic value from the premium results in the time value of $2.

52. **B)** Regulation SHO defines a threshold security as "an aggregate fail to deliver position for five consecutive settlement days at a registered clearing agency of 10,000 shares or more, and that is equal to at least 0.5% of the issue's total shares outstanding."

53. **C)** Regulation SHO stipulates that "short sales effected by a market maker in connection with bona fide market-making activities in the security" are excepted from the requirement to

54. **D)** Regulation T, Section 220.12 requires a 50% margin for short stock, for a total of 200% equity including the proceeds from the sale of the shares.

55. **C)** The market value of the separate account determines the value of an annuity unit for a variable annuity.

56. **C)** The redemption price received for mutual funds is the bid or net asset value (NAV) on the day the redemption is traded/processed. Some brokerages may process redemptions on the same day they are requested. Others may process them on the next business day. The NAV is generally determined against the price of the constituent assets at the close of the day's trading.

57. **C)** Equipment trust certificates (ETCs) are issued by companies, known as common contract carriers, and collateralized by equipment owned by the company.

58. **B)** Because XYZ Securities is under the ownership control of General Conglomerate Corp, this relationship must be disclosed to the client.

59. **D)** Level I access only shows real-time quotes but does not reveal market depth or how many shares the market maker wants.

60. **C)** The customer must pay the execution price of the stock.

61. **D)** A corporate bond is higher risk than a government bond and can be issued by any corporation. Because of its higher risk versus Treasurys, the corporate bond typically has a higher interest rate.

62. **B)** Share certificates must be divisible into groups of round lots (totaling 100 shares or a multiple thereof) and an odd lot (totaling less than 100 shares) for delivery. A single 525-share certificate (Option A) is incorrect because the delivered certificate groups the round lots with the odd lot (also known as a "mixed lot" or "partial round lot"). Each pair of 50-share certificates (Option B) constitutes a round lot, which makes for good delivery. Bonds must be delivered in good condition. Defaced or mutilated bonds (Option C) and bonds with the incorrect number of coupons (Option D) may not be delivered without additional endorsement by the trustee, registrar, transfer agent, or issuer.

63. **C)** Form 144 is effective for 90 days.

64. **D)** Treasury stock refers to the shares that a company keeps in its own treasury. These shares do not pay dividends, do not have voting rights, and are not included in calculations of shares outstanding.

65. **B)** Automobile stocks are considered cyclical stocks because of their dependence on the business cycle.

66. **B)** A rollover of assets from an employer-sponsored retirement plan to a rollover IRA must be accomplished within 60 days to avoid incurring a penalty for early withdrawal of funds.

67. **B)** The asking price, or ask, is the public offering price (POP). The bid price is the net asset value (NAV). Use the formula (POP − NAV) ÷ POP = SC%.

    POP = $16
    NAV = $15
    ($16 − $15) ÷ $16
    = $1 ÷ $16
    = 0.0625 or 6.25%

68. **B)** It may be assumed that the customer holds $1,000 in total face value of these bonds. The customer will make $80 ($1,000 − $920) upon maturity in 20 years, or $4 per year. The annual interest payment on the 9.0% bond is $90, so the adjusted interest is $94 ($90 + $4). The customer bought the bond for $920. It will mature at $1,000, so the average price is $960. The approximate yield to maturity is the adjusted interest divided by the average price. This is $94 divided by $960, which equals 9.79%.

69. **B)** Because the firm is acting in an advisory relationship to ACME Mfg. Corp., any information obtained as a result may not be used without prior written permission.

70. **B)** A hypothetical illustration of performance for a variable annuity (and other variable insurance contracts) must show a rate of return of 0% and may show any additional return up to a maximum of 12%, provided the rates illustrated are reasonable in relation to the market and available investment options.

71. **A)** American depositary receipts (ADRs) are certificates issued by a US bank that represent a specific number of shares in a foreign stock and are traded on a US exchange.

72. **B)** This is an example of interpositioning. A third party that provides no service collects a commission in this customer transaction.

73. **A)** If a bridge collapses during construction, the city will invoke the catastrophe call to use insurance proceeds to pay for the bonds.

74. **C)** In a long margin account, the minimum requirement under Regulation T is 50% of the long market value, or $2,000, which is the initial minimum requirement. In this transaction, the customer would be required to deposit $1,600 or 100% of the long market value. (The customer would not be required to deposit more than the value of the securities.)

75. **B)** The Tax Reform Act of 1986 removed many of the shelter aspects of limited partnership investments, placing a greater emphasis on the pass-through of income.

76. **A)** Information regarding a trade involving a customer and stock taken from the firm's inventory that does not take place on the floor of an exchange must be reported within 90 seconds of the trade.

77. **B)** The settlement for US Treasury bonds and notes is the trade date plus 1 business day (T + 1). Corporate and municipal bonds settle regular way T + 2, the same as common stock. Cash settlement is always the same day.

78. **A)** The enforcement of Municipal Securities Rulemaking Board (MSRB) municipal regulations for broker-dealers is overseen by FINRA. The MSRB is a rule-making body only.

79. **A)** An underwriting is the distribution of a new issue of securities.

80. **C)** Brokers, dealers, banks, and general circulation newspapers are exempt from the requirements of registering as investment advisers in accordance with the Investment Advisers Act of 1940.

81. **D)** All listed options stop trading at 3 p.m. central time (4 p.m. eastern time) on the date of their expiration.

82. **D)** Program trading is trading that is performed by computers based on predetermined conditions.

83. **D)** There is no requirement for the issuer to file an official statement with the Municipal Securities Rulemaking Board (MSRB) before an offering, as there may be pricing information in the official statement that cannot be known until after issuance. However, regulations require underwriters to send a copy of the preliminary (draft) official statement, if one is available, by the next business day after a request from a potential customer. The preliminary official statement is used when soliciting interest in a new offering, and it must be updated when new material information becomes available in order to make it as close to the final official statement as possible.

84. **D)** The municipal securities representative expressed concerns about the suitability of the transaction with the client, and the client insisted that the trade take place anyway. The representative should proceed with the execution of the order.

85. **D)** Indicative quotes are given as a reasonable estimate for informative purposes only. They are not firm quotes and are not required to be honored by the trader or his institution. Backing away would require the quote to have been firm. Front-running would require the trader to sell TUV stock for himself or his institution

while he has the customer's limit order in hand. Spoofing would require the trader to place bogus limit orders with the intention of altering other market participants' perception of supply or demand. The customer may be disappointed, but the trader's actions are lawful.

86. **C)** Municipal securities trading in the secondary market may not be purchased from the issuer.

87. **C)** Bonds with long maturities tend to be more susceptible to a decrease in interest rates than bonds with short maturities. Low-coupon bonds are more sensitive to changes in yield than high-coupon bonds.

88. **B)** A floor broker is only permitted to trade on an agency basis and cannot trade on their own behalf.

89. **C)** Corporate bonds have the lowest risk to capital (as most debt securities do) and would provide the customer with a priority claim on assets upon dissolution of the company during a bankruptcy proceeding.

90. **D)** New issuances of municipal bonds tend to have a settlement period between 2 days and 2 weeks. A municipal bond with a long settlement date of 6 weeks or more is called a forward-delivery municipal bond. Its buyer is subject to the bond's price risk, but neither receives interest accrual nor makes a cash outlay until settlement occurs.

91. **A)** When an order for municipal securities is received, the firm is required only to make every reasonable effort to obtain a fair and reasonable price.

92. **A)** Dark pools are a form of alternative trading system (ATS) and are required to comply with the standards and practices set forth in Regulation ATS. Short selling is addressed by Regulation SHO. Trading halts are addressed by FINRA Rules 6120 and 6121. Research reports are addressed by Regulation AC.

93. **B)** Because the customer expressed a price ($25) for the purchase of the stock, this is a limit order.

94. **A)** A long straddle position is established when a put and a call of the same underlying security are purchased simultaneously with the same expiration and strike price. A short straddle position is established when a put and a call of the same underlying security are sold simultaneously with the same expiration and strike price.

95. **B)** Municipal securities trade over the counter (OTC) and are not listed on the NASDAQ.

96. **D)** Long-term equity anticipation securities (LEAPS) can expire 3 or more years in the future, typically no more than 39 months.

97. **D)** FINRA Rule 4513 requires that written customer complaint records be preserved for at least 4 years.

98. **A)** A limit order enables the investor to specify the price at which she wants to buy or sell the stock. It is not guaranteed to execute and does not enable the investor to fill her order as soon as the market opens.

99. **D)** The expiration date for equity options is technically the Saturday after the third Friday of the month in which the options are scheduled to expire.

100. **C)** The hypothecation of customer securities to finance a debit balance is permitted under the Securities Act of 1933.

101. **D)** The total volume for the past 4 weeks was 135,000 shares (30,000 + 40,000 + 35,000 + 30,000) for an average weekly volume of 33,750. This is less than 1% of the shares outstanding, which is 40,000 shares. The company president may sell 40,000 shares, which is the greater of 1% of the shares outstanding or the 4-week average weekly volume under the restrictions of Rule 144.

102. **A)** Those who wish to sell restricted or control securities must receive an exemption from the SEC to sell them publicly. Rule 144 allows resale under certain conditions and limitations.

103. **B)** Because the order is placed before 3:45 p.m. to sell at market-on-close, it will receive a price determined during the closing auction.

104. **C)** A redemption notice is used to call all or part of an outstanding redeemable security (such as bonds, notes, or preferred stock).

105. **B)** A stop-loss order is also known as a "stop order" or "stop-market order" and is placed with a broker to sell a security when the security reaches a certain price. Execution is not guaranteed.

106. **C)** The FINRA 5% markup policy addresses a variety of situations including agency-only transactions, dealer sales from firm inventory, dealer purchases of securities from customers, and facilitated orders.

107. **D)** Tombstone ads are neither an offer to sell nor a solicitation to buy. They condition the market for a transaction by providing basic facts.

108. **B)** This is a violation of FINRA rules. Representatives are not permitted to guarantee against customer losses.

109. **D)** A put option is in-the-money when the market price is below the strike price. When the market price is less than $30, the long put will be in-the-money.

110. **B)** In a firm commitment underwriting, the underwriting firm must purchase all of the securities from the issuer regardless of whether the underwriting firm can sell them. In doing so, the firm takes on risk. A firm commitment underwriting is desirable for the issuer of the securities. Option A describes a standby underwriting. Option C describes a best efforts underwriting.

111. **C)** A short straddle profits from selling a call and a put with the same expiration date and strike price. This strategy works best in a neutral or sideways market where volatility realizes less than anticipated.

112. **C)** Intrinsic value is the amount that an option is in-the-money. A call is in-the-money when the market price of the underlying security is above the strike price. A put is in-the-money when the market price of the underlying security is below the strike price, regardless of whether the call or put is bought (held) or sold (written). Option A refers to the options time value, which is the premium portion of the intrinsic value (intrinsic value minus premium = time value).

113. **A)** Exploratory oil and gas wells are drilled in unproven fields, typically away from a producing development well.

114. **C)** The 200,000 shares of repurchased stock (Treasury stock) are a secondary offering. The new shares are a primary offering. Because this offering includes both a primary distribution and a secondary distribution, it is called a split offering.

115. **A)** Time and demand deposits are the banking activities of commercial retail banks, not investment banks.

116. **C)** Stock option exercises settle regular way, which is T + 2. They are no different from trades made on an exchange in this regard.

117. **A)** An immediate-or-cancel order is an immediate market execution that may result in a partial fill. Remaining shares not filled will be canceled.

118. **D)** The tombstone ad only provides information about a securities offering. It is not an offer to buy or sell shares.

119. **B)** An order to buy market-on-close is executed in the closing auction of the day. The guaranteed execution deadline for market-on-close orders is 3:45 p.m. for the NYSE.

120. **A)** The buy limit order would be reduced by $0.55 to $39.45.

121. **D)** Time and price discretion is a stipulation of FINRA Rule 3260. If a written authorization is not available, a customer may give his broker time and price discretion for a trade on the same day to buy (or sell) a definite amount of a security.

122. **A)** This trade is a buy-write. Since it has no net risk on the upside, its breakeven is the point at

which a decline in the stock offsets the premium collected from the sale of the option, or $22 ($30 − $8).

123. **C)** Stock splits and stock dividends generally increase the number of shares while decreasing the exercise price.

124. **C)** It would be difficult for a limited partnership to avoid the centralization of management because this business structure concentrates control of operations and business decisions in the hands of the general partners.

125. **A)** If the issuer of the securities is subject to reporting requirements under the Exchange Act, a minimum of 6 months must pass from the date of the acquisition to the date of the resale of the securities.

126. **B)** If the stock market is consolidating, it is trading in a narrow range, and the trend line will be sideways.

127. **D)** The notation *ZR* stands for "zero-coupon bond."

128. **C)** An all-or-none order is an order to buy multiple round lots at a set price when the customer is willing to wait for full execution at the chosen price or better.

129. **D)** In-the-money American-style call options are typically exercised before an ex-dividend date when their remaining time value (premium in excess of intrinsic value) is less than the amount of the dividend. Long holders have a financial incentive to exercise and collect the dividend rather than holding a lesser amount of time value. The 31 call has no intrinsic value, and the 30 and 29 calls have more time value than the dividend. Based on its offer price, the 28 call only has a maximum of 60 cents of time value, so a long holder would prefer to exercise and collect the dividend of 70 cents. This decision results in a marginal profit of at least $10.00 per contract.

130. **A)** Arbitration is generally less costly than litigation.

131. **B)** Uncovered call writing is the most speculative position because its losses are unbounded. In contrast, a short spread has defined risk, and a long call cannot lose more than the premium outlay.

132. **A)** The customer received $800 in premiums through the sale of the call and the put in this short straddle. Upon exercise of the put, he was under an obligation to purchase DEF stock for $40 per share from the put's holder. Since the customer was only able to sell the stock at $35 per share, he experienced a net loss of $500 on the stock transaction; however, the $800 gain in premium collected nets against the loss on the shares for a total of $300 profit.

133. **C)** Intangible drilling costs are the primary deduction available in an oil and gas drilling partnership in the first year. In fact, they are one of the largest tax deductions available specifically to oil companies.

134. **A)** The time between the filing of the registration statement and its effective date is the cooling-off period, which typically lasts 20 days.

135. **B)** A customer account with a free credit balance is required to receive account statements at least quarterly.

2 Practice Test 2

1. A FINRA member prepares an investment-related research report for distribution to institutional investors. The FINRA member has recently become aware that many recipients of its research reports redistribute them to retail customers, so it clearly marks the report as "For Institutional Use Only." Is the FINRA member required to follow guidelines for retail communications for this report?

   A) No, because the FINRA member is not directly sending the report to retail customers.
   B) No, because the report is explicitly marked as "For Institutional Use Only."
   C) Yes, because there is reason to believe that retail customers will receive the report.
   D) Yes, because all institutional communications must meet the standard for retail communications.

2. An option investor sold a cash-secured LMNO Dec 50-strike put contract at a premium of $3 when LMNO stock was trading at $52. On Dec expiry, LMNO stock closed at $48, an all-time low for the stock. Assuming no other trades are made, what is the option investor's profit or loss?

   A) $100 gain
   B) $100 loss
   C) $200 loss
   D) $400 loss

3. EFG Corp. issues a zero-coupon 3-year bond with a yield to maturity of 1%. How is this bond priced?

   A) at a discount
   B) at a premium
   C) at par
   D) There is insufficient information to answer the question.

4. A bond investor considers purchasing a 6-year corporate bond with a face value of $10,000 that pays an annual coupon of 7.00%. This bond is offered in the market at $14,000. What is its current yield?

   A) 0.27%
   B) 0.71%
   C) 5.00%
   D) 7.00%

5. Stock TUV trades ex-dividend tomorrow and closes at exactly $55.00 this afternoon. An investor has a portfolio containing the following four American-style options positions. Which of these options should she consider exercising early, in order to collect the $0.20 dividend?

   A) long TUV Dec 55 put
   B) long TUV Oct 60 call
   C) long TUV Jul 30 call
   D) short TUV Jul 25 call

6. Which of the following bonds offers a payout that is linked to the rate of inflation?
   A) MBS
   B) STRIPS
   C) TIGRs
   D) TIPS

7. From the perspective of a bond investor, which of the following is never an advantage of a sinking-fund provision in a bond indenture?
   A) smooth retirement of debt
   B) optional acceleration feature
   C) price stability
   D) enhancement of secondary market liquidity

8. A municipal securities advertisement from a broker-dealer to an institutional investor is subject to MSRB rules. When and how does it need to be approved?
   A) never
   B) before first use, in writing by a registered principal
   C) before first use, in writing by a registered representative
   D) before first use, in writing by the recipient

9. What is the common term for a preliminary prospectus for a securities offering that has been submitted to the SEC but not yet approved?
   A) red herring
   B) shelf prospectus
   C) straw man
   D) greenshoe

10. A brokerage designated a customer as a pattern day trader for executing 6 day trades in his margin account last week. What is the minimum equity that he is now required to maintain in his account?
    A) $2,000
    B) $10,000
    C) $20,000
    D) $25,000

11. An institutional customer has exclusively traded US-listed bank stocks for the past 3 years. On Monday morning, the customer submits an order to buy a large quantity of a commodity ETF for $100 per share. The broker-dealer executes this order. In the afternoon, the customer submits an order to short-sell the same quantity of the commodity ETF in a separate account at $100 per share. What course of action should the broker-dealer take?
    A) execute the order as usual and take no further action
    B) execute the order as usual and immediately submit a Suspicious Activity Report
    C) refuse to execute the order and immediately submit a Suspicious Activity Report
    D) refuse to execute the order until additional due diligence is performed

12. Which of the following municipal securities offerings may require preparation of an official statement?
    A) a new issue with a total size of $700,000
    B) a new issue distributed to thirty institutional investors, with $1 million allocated to each
    C) a new issue maturing in 6 months, totaling $30 million divided equally among two investors
    D) a new issue maturing in 10 years, with $50,000 allocated to each of sixty institutional investors

13. YZ Corp. has two kinds of outstanding 10-year bonds, YZ Bond A and YZ Bond B, which mature on the same date and pay the same semiannual coupon of 2%. Both bonds have a face value of $100. The bond indentures for these two bonds are identical except for one difference: YZ Bond A is callable at face value, and YZ Bond B is noncallable. An investor asks his broker which of these bonds is worth more. How should the broker respond?
    A) YZ Bond A is worth strictly more than YZ Bond B.
    B) YZ Bond B is worth strictly more than YZ Bond A.
    C) YZ Bond A is worth exactly the same as YZ Bond B.
    D) The answer to the investor's question will change based on market conditions.

14. An investor holds a long Sep 38 call on GHIJ stock, which is currently offered at $37.22. He wants to turn his position into a long strangle because he anticipates future volatility, but he lacks an opinion about the direction of the spot price. Which of the following contracts can he purchase to accomplish his goal?

    A) Aug 40 call
    B) Sep 38 put
    C) Aug 36 put
    D) Sep 36 put

15. Townsville City issues a municipal bond to build a new oceanside water park. The bond's trust indenture specifies that all revenue from ticket sales will be set aside and used to repay bondholders. If ticket revenue falls short of expectations and is insufficient to cover repayment of the debt, the full faith and credit of Townsville City will make up the difference. This is an example of what kind of bond?

    A) general obligation (GO) bond
    B) revenue bond
    C) double-barreled bond
    D) faith and credit bond

16. A broker makes periodic tailored recommendations to its customers who hold retirement accounts. Which of the following is the broker NOT required to consider when determining the suitability of an investment for a particular customer?

    A) the customer's willingness to act on the broker's investment recommendations
    B) the extent to which the customer may need to readily convert all holdings to cash
    C) the number of years remaining before the customer expects to retire
    D) the customer's ability to take additional risk in pursuit of greater returns

17. Which of the following is a debt security that divides the cash flows from a pool of mortgages pro-rata among its holders?

    A) pass-through mortgage-backed security (MBS)
    B) collateralized mortgage obligation (CMO)
    C) asset-backed security (ABS)
    D) collateralized debt obligation (CDO)

18. UVW Incorporated has a 50-year 8.0% bond outstanding, with a current yield of 4.0% and a face value of $100. If the bond's market price drops by 20.0%, what is the new current yield of this UVW 8.0% bond?

    A) 3.2%
    B) 4.0%
    C) 4.8%
    D) 5.0%

19. A registered representative who trades equities for a risk desk is filling out an order ticket to electronically purchase 10,000 shares of BCD stock for her firm. After she has filled out the ticket but before routing it to an exchange, she receives a customer market order to buy a block of 100,000 shares of BCD. May she submit her own order?

    A) Yes, she is not permitted to alter her trades due to nonpublic information about customer orders.
    B) Yes, she filled out the ticket in good faith before she knew about the customer order.
    C) No, the registered representative cannot trade in front of the live customer order for BCD stock.
    D) Yes, but she must inform the customer and receive the customer's authorization first.

20. VWXY stock is trading at $24.00. It pays a quarterly dividend of $0.30. What is its dividend yield?

    A) 1.25%
    B) 5.00%
    C) 8.00%
    D) 30.00%

21. A registered representative notices that an elderly customer has put all of her discretionary account's equity into the stock of NOP Corp., a pharmaceutical company with a single experimental drug. What must the registered representative do before he can liquidate NOP and diversify the account's holdings?

    A) No additional steps are required.
    B) Verbal authorization is required.
    C) Written authorization is required.
    D) Liquidation is not permitted.

22. A grandmother gives a gift of securities totaling $20,000 to her grandson. This gift is taxable for
    A) the grandson.
    B) the grandmother.
    C) both.
    D) neither.

23. What is the minimum frequency for account statements to be delivered to the holder of an account wherein securities are actively traded?
    A) annually
    B) semiannually
    C) quarterly
    D) monthly

24. The QRS Jan 44 put had an open interest of zero on Monday, and it has traded only twice this week. On Tuesday, a hedge fund bought 700 QRS Jan 44 put contracts from an investment bank. On Wednesday, the same account at that investment bank bought 500 QRS Jan 44 put contracts from an asset manager. Today is Thursday. What is the open interest?
    A) 200
    B) 500
    C) 700
    D) 1,200

25. A member firm terminates its association with a registered representative for reasons that do not involve a statutory disqualification. Within how many calendar days must the member firm notify FINRA of this change to the registered representative's status?
    A) 1
    B) 7
    C) 10
    D) 30

26. Which of the following is NOT generally considered a fully amortizing loan?
    A) home equity loan
    B) personal loan
    C) balloon mortgage
    D) vehicle loan

27. A customer opens a Regulation T margin account and funds it with $9,000. For his first trade, he buys twenty shares of PQRS stock for $800 each. A week later, PQRS reports accounting irregularities, and the stock falls overnight to $400. At LEAST how much additional margin must the customer post with his brokerage in order to meet maintenance requirements?
    A) $1,000
    B) $2,000
    C) $3,000
    D) $4,000

28. A customer who is bullish about the prospects of JKL Corp., trading at $52.00, buys 20 Sep 55 call options for $4.50 each. When the closing bell rings on Sep expiration, JKL stock has rallied 10% from where it was trading. The customer exercises all of his call options. What is his profit or loss?
    A) $10,400 loss
    B) $4,600 loss
    C) $4,600 gain
    D) $10,400 gain

29. STUV Industries issues a 6-year bond with a semiannual coupon of 1.5% in the first 5 years and 2.0% in the sixth year. It is callable after 3 years. What kind of bond is this?
    A) equipment trust certificate
    B) nonrefundable bond
    C) step-up bond
    D) collateralized debt obligation

30. An investor's account at Brokerage A contains four holdings. She wants to transfer all of her holdings to Brokerage B using the Automated Customer Account Transfer Service (ACATS), but Brokerage A says this is impossible due to one of her holdings. Which of the following holdings in her account CANNOT be transferred via ACATS?
    A) mutual fund available at both Brokerages A and B
    B) master limited partnership
    C) annuity
    D) investment-grade corporate bond

31. The exchange-traded fund FGH closed last week at $100. Returns of FGH strongly correlate to those of the SPX Index, with a beta of −1.5. If SPX has fallen by 2% since the close of trading last week, what could the current price of FGH be?
    A) $96.50
    B) $97.00
    C) $103.00
    D) $103.50

32. The stock of DEF Mfg. trades at $70.00. Due to excellent management, DEF's earnings per share have been consistent at $0.35 per quarter for the past 4 years. What is the company's P/E ratio?
    A) 2
    B) 5
    C) 20
    D) 50

33. Which of the following forms of debt service are tax-deductible?
    A) corporate interest payments
    B) consumer interest payments
    C) both corporate and consumer interest payments
    D) neither corporate nor consumer interest payments

34. A US corporate bond trader is calculating accrued interest from January 29 to March 2 during a leap year. How many days should he attribute to February?
    A) 27
    B) 28
    C) 30
    D) 31

35. An options investor speculating on JKL stock buys a Sep 30 call for $3.00, sells 2 Sep 35 calls at $1.20, and buys a Sep 40 call for $0.40. This strategy has two break-even levels, and one of them is $39.00. What is the other breakeven?
    A) $30.40
    B) $31.00
    C) $34.00
    D) $48.00

36. A retiree invests $1 million into a mutual fund with a POP of $10.00, a sales charge of $0.50 per share, and an MER of 2%. A year later, the NAV has not changed, so the retiree decides to close her position and deploy the capital elsewhere. The mutual fund has no redemption fee. How much money does the retiree recoup from the mutual fund by closing her stake?
    A) $931,000
    B) $950,000
    C) $980,000
    D) $1,000,000

37. A block of exchange-listed equity securities trades on an ATS. When must the transaction be reported and to whom?
    A) within 15 minutes to TRACE
    B) within 15 minutes to a TRF
    C) within 10 seconds to TRACE
    D) within 10 seconds to a TRF

38. A bondholder decides to exercise a provision in a CDE Materials Corp. bond that he owns. This provision forces the issuer to accelerate the payout to the bondholder and terminate the debt. The issuer delivers the payout in the form of CDE common stock. What was the nature of the provision exercised by the bondholder?
    A) soft call
    B) hard call
    C) soft put
    D) hard put

39. Which of the following individuals is likely NOT an accredited investor?
    A) a painter who owns an art collection worth $10 million and has no other assets or any debt
    B) a bond saleswoman who holds Series 7 and Series 65 licenses
    C) an engineer who earns $160,000 annually and is married to a person who earns the same
    D) an engineer who earns $180,000 annually and is unmarried, with a net worth under $1 million

40. In which of the following transaction methods would a security change hands immediately when (or immediately after) payment is made?

   A) delivery versus free
   B) delivery versus payment
   C) cash settlement
   D) delivery versus delivery

41. The date of record for the quarterly dividend paid to holders of GHI stock, which trades on the New York Stock Exchange, falls on Thursday of this week. Assuming no holidays, what is the latest day this week that an investor can buy GHI stock and receive the dividend?

   A) Monday
   B) Tuesday
   C) Wednesday
   D) Thursday

42. A customer with a margin account files a formal written complaint to Brokerage Q. She claims that her positions are being incorrectly liquidated despite her account's equity meeting all margin requirements. Brokerage Q investigates and finds that the customer is mistaken; all processes have been correctly followed in liquidating her margined securities. Brokerage Q communicates this to the customer and stores the complaint and investigation results in the relevant office. How long must this information be preserved?

   A) 60 days
   B) 90 days
   C) 4 years
   D) 5 years

43. An equities investor wants to understand the theoretical value of warrants that will be granted to shareholders of XYZ Company, in which his firm holds a large equity stake. His firm lacks a pricing tool intended specifically for use with warrants, but he can use any of the four following tools. Which would be most useful?

   A) option pricer
   B) futures pricer
   C) bond pricer
   D) swaps pricer

44. An immediate-or-cancel order to buy 600 shares of a very illiquid security crosses with a fill-or-kill limit order to sell 500 shares of the security. Do these orders transact, and if so, how many shares does the buyer receive?

   A) no; 0 shares
   B) yes; 500 shares
   C) yes; 600 shares
   D) yes; 1,100 shares

45. Transactions in which of the following securities are reported to the Real-Time Transaction Reporting System?

   A) municipal securities
   B) equity securities
   C) Treasury bonds
   D) corporate bonds

46. A customer wants to make a contribution to a Coverdell ESA for her ten-year-old nephew Thomas, whose mother already made a $500 contribution this year. What is the maximum amount she can contribute to the account for Thomas?

   A) $500
   B) $1,000
   C) $1,500
   D) $2,000

47. A customer wants to open an IRA, but he does not know if he would be better served by a traditional IRA or a Roth IRA. He typically earns a taxable income of more than $1 million a year, but he lives well below his means. He plans to spend his retirement gardening and building birdhouses, with a very modest cost of living, in a residence he already owns. Is there a clearly preferable option for him?

   A) Yes, a traditional IRA is preferable.
   B) Yes, a Roth IRA is preferable.
   C) No, both IRA categories are equally beneficial.
   D) Not enough information is provided.

48. A customer has $2,700 to invest, so she buys $900 worth of WXYZ stock every Tuesday for 3 weeks. The net price of a share of WXYZ stock in each of those transactions is $15.00, $30.00, and $45.00, respectively. What is the customer's average price per share?

    A) $24.55
    B) $27.50
    C) $29.43
    D) $30.00

49. A customer is new to the securities markets and wants to buy 100 shares of a $2 penny stock for his first transaction. This is permitted

    A) under no circumstances.
    B) after the broker vets and verifies the customer's proficiency with penny stocks.
    C) after the broker provides the customer with a Risk Disclosure Document.
    D) after the customer acknowledges receipt of a Risk Disclosure Document in writing.

50. A 10-year corporate bond with a par value of $1,000 pays a 12% annual coupon rate. It is offered in the US bond market at $1,730. Since the last coupon payment, this bond has accrued interest for 5 days in October, all of November, all of December, and 7 days in January. What is the bond's dirty price?

    A) $1,730
    B) $1,754
    C) $1,759
    D) $1,760

51. The stock of KLMN & Co. is illiquid, heavily shorted, and hard to borrow. A market maker with no existing position in the stock receives a customer buy order for 30,000 shares of KLMN, but she locates borrow for only 25,000 shares. According to Regulation SHO, how many shares can the market maker sell to the customer?

    A) 0
    B) 25,000
    C) 27,500
    D) 30,000

52. The NYSE has recently listed MNO shares, which have traded with a volume of four million shares today. An overzealous trader places a limit-on-close buy order for forty million shares of MNO, with a limit price of $106. The last consolidated sale of MNO before the closing auction trades at exactly $100. What is the highest price at which the trader's order may transact?

    A) $100
    B) $101
    C) $105
    D) $106

53. A customer has owned 1,000 shares of UVW stock for 20 years. Each month, he sells 10 UVW 1-month call options with a strike price at least 5% higher than the last price of UVW. Which of the following BEST describes the customer's call-selling strategy?

    A) speculation
    B) arbitrage
    C) hedging
    D) yield enhancement

54. Who is allowed to participate in a Rule 144A offering?

    A) an accredited investor
    B) a qualified institutional buyer
    C) a customer approved to trade penny stocks
    D) a sophisticated investor

55. Which of the following is NOT a characteristic of American depositary receipts (ADRs)?

    A) denomination in a foreign currency
    B) listing on a domestic exchange
    C) the potential for double taxation of dividends
    D) access to foreign equity markets

56. An REIT can distribute a majority of its income from any of the following pools of assets EXCEPT

    A) construction loans.
    B) network tower rents.
    C) collateralized mortgage obligations (CMOs).
    D) auto loans.

57. An option investor with no preexisting position buys a Jan/Feb 25-strike call calendar spread for $2.20. The underlier, WXY stock, closed at $24.00 on Jan expiry. Assuming the option investor liquidates her position for parity when WXY trades $28.00 on Feb expiry, what is her profit or loss?

   A) $80
   B) $120
   C) $220
   D) $300

58. A bond trader is quoted by two separate customers for a firm offer on ABC Corp.'s 30-year 4% bond. He communicates a bond price of $1 million to both customers. Customer A quickly says, "mine." Five minutes later, Customer B responds that he wants all $1 million of the offer. Assuming no other communications and no other transactions, what should the bond trader do?

   A) sell $1 million of the bond to Customer A and tell Customer B that the offer has already traded
   B) sell $1 million of the bond to Customer A and offer an updated price to Customer B
   C) sell $1 million of the bond to Customer A and $1 million to Customer B
   D) sell $500,000 of the bond to Customer A and $500,000 to Customer B

59. Stock TUVW encounters resistance near $70 and reverts as a result. How can the current price be described?

   A) above $70
   B) equal to $70
   C) below $70
   D) not enough information provided

60. Which of the following corporations is wholly owned by the US government?

   A) Ginnie Mae
   B) Freddie Mac
   C) Fannie Mae
   D) Farmer Mac

61. A customer buys an in-the-money call option on Monday. When that option purchase settles, the customer immediately exercises the option to buy 100 shares of stock. When that exercise transaction settles, the customer immediately sells all 100 shares at market. Assuming no holidays, on what day can the customer expect all of the proceeds from this series of transactions to have settled in her account?

   A) Monday
   B) Wednesday
   C) Thursday
   D) Friday

62. A securities broker sends two gifts every year to his client, one for the client's wedding anniversary and another for Christmas. This year, the broker sent a bottle of wine valued at $88 on the client's anniversary. How much is he allowed to spend on the Christmas gift at maximum?

   A) $12
   B) $62
   C) $100
   D) $150

63. Which of the following debt securities is used to finance the purchase of aircraft?

   A) CMO
   B) ETC
   C) DAL
   D) REIT

64. A large bank owns considerable amounts of stock in all constituents of SPY, a very liquid exchange-traded fund (ETF), and wants to convert its holdings into SPY shares. Assuming the bank is an authorized participant and that the number of shares is sufficiently large, which transaction would most efficiently accomplish the bank's wishes?

   A) creation
   B) redemption
   C) reverse conversion
   D) tender offer

65. A member firm's operations team receives a trade confirmation for a security that the firm traded on the trade date shown but not at the price and quantity specified. How should the member firm respond?

   A) accept and book the trade as confirmed
   B) submit a request for quotation
   C) contrary exercise
   D) don't know

66. OPQ Corp. files a registration statement for an initial public offering that is subsequently approved by the SEC. How long must the executives of OPQ wait after the stock begins trading publicly before they can disclose new information to potential buyers of OPQ stock?

   A) 15 days
   B) 20 days
   C) 40 days
   D) 90 days

67. SEC and FINRA rules require securities brokers to deliver an options disclosure document to customers before they do which of the following?

   A) open an option account
   B) effect an options trade
   C) sell an option contract
   D) sell an option contract short

68. The initial public offering of EFG Corp. is underwritten on a firm-commitment basis, but the underwriters are only able to sell 75% of the issue. EFG was seeking to raise $100 million from the IPO. How much does EFG actually raise?

   A) $25 million
   B) $50 million
   C) $75 million
   D) $100 million

69. An options investor notices that the put/call volume ratio for TUVW stock is above 1.0 this week. What can the investor safely conclude?

   A) TUVW stock is expected to decline.
   B) More calls than puts have traded this week.
   C) More puts than calls have traded this week.
   D) TUVW stock is expected to appreciate.

70. A young professional decides to roll over her entire Roth 401(k) to a Roth IRA that she has set up specifically for this purpose. She chooses to set up this transaction in the form of a trustee-to-trustee transfer. How much of the balance will be withheld for taxes and penalties?

   A) 0%
   B) 10%
   C) 20%
   D) 25%

71. A bond trader wants to buy an investment-grade 30-year bond. He requests quotations from four dealers who respond with the following four offers, each quoted as a spread to the benchmark 30-year Treasury bond. From the perspective of the bond trader, which is the BEST offer?

   A) 69 bps
   B) 0.71%
   C) 0.73%
   D) 74 bps

72. After a registration statement is filed for an initial public offering, the SEC mandates a 20-day waiting period wherein certain activities relating to the IPO are prohibited. Which activity is permitted during the waiting period?

   A) sale of the offered security
   B) solicitation of indications of interest
   C) disclosure of new information about the company
   D) acceptance of deposits for a future sale of the security

73. FGH Industries has one million shares of common stock outstanding, no preferred stock outstanding, and outstanding debt with a face value of $100 million. This debt was issued as a single zero-coupon bond priced at $80, and it has accrued $15 of interest. FGH Industries files for Chapter 7 bankruptcy, and its liquidation proceeds are $110 million. How much does FGH common stock pay out?

   A) $0
   B) $5
   C) $15
   D) $85

74. From its date of issuance, how long might a Treasury note take to mature?
    A) 1 year
    B) 7 years
    C) 20 years
    D) 30 years

75. If a customer purchases ABC common stock in a regular-way settlement on Thursday, October 7, what is the settlement date for the transaction?
    A) Friday, October 8
    B) Monday, October 11
    C) Tuesday, October 12
    D) Friday, October 15

76. Bank G sells a 5-year Treasury note 2 days before its auction takes place. Which of the following terms BEST describes this transaction?
    A) front-running
    B) ex-rights
    C) gun-jumping
    D) when-issued

77. A member firm owns 10,000 BCD Sep 50 call contracts and has hedged these contracts by shorting one million shares of BCD at an average price of $59.55. On Sep expiration, BCD stock closes at exactly $50.00. Assuming no other trades and exercise-by-exception processing, what will the member firm's BCD share position be on the following Monday morning?
    A) short one million shares of BCD
    B) short 500,000 shares of BCD
    C) no long or short shares of BCD
    D) long one million shares of BCD

78. A FINRA member routes customer orders to another broker-dealer for execution on an automated, nondiscretionary basis. How frequently is the member required to review the execution quality of this arrangement to ensure that the other broker-dealer is upholding the requirement of best execution for the customer?
    A) at least weekly
    B) at least monthly
    C) at least quarterly
    D) at least annually

79. A trade confirmation statement says that an option was purchased for $5.30 on the Chicago Board of Exchange (CBOE). Two hours later, the CBOE sends a notice that the original confirmation was erroneous and the true price transacted was $5.40, or $10.00 worse for the customer per contract. The buy order's limit price was $5.50. At what price will the customer's fill be honored?
    A) $5.30
    B) $5.35
    C) $5.40
    D) $5.50

80. A FINRA member requests information from a prospective customer who seeks to open a brokerage account. What information must be received and recorded before opening the new account?
    A) whether the customer is an associated person of another member firm
    B) the customer's social security number
    C) the customer's occupation
    D) the customer's residence

81. Which of the following securities would be considered to have defaulted if periodic distributions are not paid according to schedule?
    A) income bond
    B) revenue bond
    C) subordinated debenture
    D) cumulative preferred stock

82. Stock ABC is expected to be extremely volatile for the next 3 months. Stock XYZ is in the same sector but is expected not to be very volatile over that same period. Both stocks are currently trading at exactly $144.82, and neither stock pays dividends. For which of these two stocks is the 3-month 145-strike straddle more expensive?
    A) stock ABC
    B) stock XYZ
    C) They are equal.
    D) not enough information provided

83. Which of the following transactions would NOT need to be registered with the Securities and Exchange Commission?
    A) initial public offering
    B) shelf offering
    C) intrastate offering
    D) Regulation A offering

84. For which of the following securities is the current yield lower than the nominal yield?
    A) premium bond
    B) par bond
    C) discount bond
    D) original-issue Treasury bond

85. A customer plans to invest in one of the four securities issued by VWX Corp. She wants a steady distribution, and she wants to make money if VWX stock gets more expensive. However, the customer is also concerned about a legal proceeding that could bankrupt VWX Corp. She wants her investment to be as high as possible in the capital structure of VWX Corp. while continuing to satisfy the other two criteria. Which of the following securities is she MOST likely to buy?
    A) common stock
    B) mortgage bond with 3% coupon
    C) cumulative preferred stock with 1% dividend
    D) convertible bond with 1% coupon

86. A mutual fund invests almost entirely in short-term commercial paper and original issues of 6-month Treasury debt. How can its core asset class BEST be described?
    A) high yield
    B) equities
    C) money market
    D) commodities

87. A hedge fund buys 10 million dollars' worth of a corporate bond from a dealer in an over-the-counter transaction. Within what time frame must this trade be reported to TRACE?
    A) 10 seconds
    B) 10 minutes
    C) 15 minutes
    D) 60 minutes

88. A portfolio theorist is comparing two strategies: Strategy A and Strategy B. Both strategies generate the same average return when tested using historical data, but Strategy A returns exhibit a much larger standard deviation than those of Strategy B. Which strategy has a higher Sharpe ratio?
    A) Strategy A
    B) Strategy B
    C) Both strategies have the same Sharpe ratio.
    D) There is not enough information provided.

89. ABC Corp. holds $20 million in cash and owns $60 million in Treasury notes. It owns no other marketable securities, but the company has accounts receivable totaling $20 million within the upcoming 90 days. ABC Corporation also has outstanding debt of $80 million, all of which is due in 8 months. What is its acid-test ratio?
    A) 0.5
    B) 0.75
    C) 1.0
    D) 1.25

90. An options trader sells 3 QRS Oct 50-strike puts at $1.30 each when the stock is trading at $53.23. QRS stock closes at $49.20 on Oct expiry, and the put options are all assigned. Now long 300 shares, the options trader sells 3 Nov 50-strike calls at $2.00 each. QRS stock rallies to $71.20 by Nov expiry, and the Nov call options are all assigned. The options trader now has no position in QRS stock. Assuming no other trades, what is the options trader's profit?
    A) $210
    B) $330
    C) $990
    D) $6,600

91. From the investor's viewpoint, which of these securities has the greatest reinvestment risk?
    A) TUVW common stock, with a dividend yield of 4.0%
    B) TUVW 10-year bullet bond, with a current yield of 3.0%
    C) TUVW 10-year bond puttable at par, with a current yield of 2.5%
    D) TUVW 10-year bond callable at par, with a current yield of 3.5%

92. Wolfram Bridge Management, a closed-end investment company with a diversified equity portfolio, invests $3 billion of its assets in public companies that are valued at over $250 million each. Wolfram Bridge does not invest in private companies, foreign companies, or companies that are subject to a bankruptcy proceeding. Additionally, Wolfram Bridge holds no cash, no money market securities, and no real estate of its own. What is the minimum amount of capital that Wolfram Bridge must have invested in public companies valued below $250 million in order to qualify as a Business Development Company?
    A) $3 billion
    B) $6 billion
    C) $7 billion
    D) $9 billion

93. From the perspective of a bond buyer, which of the following ratings by S&P Global is high yield for a bond issue?
    A) A+
    B) B+
    C) BBB–
    D) BBB+

94. A FINRA member firm files Form U4 after hiring a salesperson. Three days later, the member firm learns that the salesperson's residential history includes one address that the firm spelled incorrectly in its filing. Assuming no statutory disqualifications are involved, within how much time (from the date of learning of the error) must the FINRA member firm update its Form U4 filing?
    A) 7 days
    B) 10 days
    C) 30 days
    D) 60 days

95. The NYSE's market-wide circuit breakers will halt trading for 15 minutes after a Level 1 or Level 2 breach. How long will trading be halted after a Level 3 breach?
    A) 15 minutes following the breach
    B) 30 minutes following the breach
    C) 90 minutes following the breach
    D) the remainder of the trading day

96. Two corporate bond dealers receive an Offer Wanted In Competition (OWIC) request for an investment-grade bond maturing in 30 years. Dealer A responds to the customer with a spread of +20 basis points (versus the market yield of a 30-year Treasury bond). Dealer B responds to the customer with a spread of +18 basis points. Which dealer would the customer prefer to trade with and why?
    A) The customer buys from Dealer A because Dealer A's price was cheaper.
    B) The customer buys from Dealer B because Dealer B's price was cheaper.
    C) The customer sells to Dealer A because Dealer A's price was richer.
    D) The customer sells to Dealer B because Dealer B's price was richer.

97. An OTC market maker shows a bid of $0.30 and an offer of $0.55 for an OTC security in an inter-dealer quotation system, with 1,000 shares on each side. The best bid and best offer in the inter-dealer quotation system are $0.30 and $0.40, respectively, with an aggregate of 10,000 shares on each side. If submitted to the OTC market maker by a customer, which of the four following orders would NOT be required to be immediately displayed?
    A) customer limit bid of 1,000 shares for $0.30
    B) customer limit offer of 900 shares at $0.45
    C) customer limit bid of 50 shares for $0.35
    D) customer limit offer of 100 shares at $0.35

98. Which of the following Treasury securities pays NO coupons?
    A) Treasury note
    B) Treasury bond
    C) Treasury bill
    D) TIPS

99. From the perspective of a bank, which of these is an advantage of bank-qualified bonds?
    A) The bonds receive favorable tax treatment.
    B) The funds raised are reinvested in the banking sector.
    C) The issuer is an investment-focused public company.
    D) The current yield is greater than that of similar nonqualified bonds.

100. Bond A features a 3% semiannual coupon and traded ex-coupon yesterday. Bond B features a 2% semiannual coupon and trades ex-coupon tomorrow. Both Bond A and Bond B are offered in the US corporate bond market at the same clean price. Which has a greater dirty price?

A) Bond A has a greater dirty price than Bond B.
B) Bond B has a greater dirty price than Bond A.
C) Bond A and Bond B have equivalent dirty prices.
D) Not enough information is provided.

101. An investment company intends to pay a cash dividend to its shareholders despite having suffered net losses in the current year. To avoid negative attention, the investment company chooses not to issue a separate written disclosure of the dividend's source of funds. According to the Investment Company Act of 1940, from which of the following sources would the investment company be permitted to pay this cash dividend?

A) wholly from net income for the previous year
B) wholly from the proceeds of the sale of an office building this year
C) wholly from the proceeds of the sale of an office building in the previous year
D) wholly from the proceeds of the sale of a single security this year

102. A Trading Permit Holder (TPH) bound by Chicago Board of Exchange margin rules has a customer who opens a long position requiring additional margin. Assuming the transaction does not involve a security futures contract, which of the following means of meeting the margin requirement is acceptable?

A) liquidation of the trade in question until the capital in the account meets margin requirements
B) liquidation of other securities until the capital in the account meets margin requirements
C) short-selling of other securities in order to offset the new long position
D) furnishing of additional margin via a wire transfer of USD cash

103. For an investment company to lawfully operate under the name XYZ Cruelty-Free Cosmetics Equity Fund, at LEAST what percent of its investments must consist of equity in cruelty-free cosmetics companies?

A) 60%
B) 70%
C) 80%
D) 90%

104. A customer instructs his brokerage firm to exercise a listed call option contract that is 2 pennies out-of-the-money and ceases trading today. What is the deadline for the brokerage firm to submit a contrary exercise advice?

A) 4:00 p.m. EST
B) 4:30 p.m. EST
C) 5:00 p.m. EST
D) 5:30 p.m. EST

105. Which of the following pairs of transactions qualifies as a wash sale according to the IRS?

A) closing sale of 10 ABC Dec 22 calls, then an opening buy of 10 ABC Dec 22 puts 4 days later
B) closing sale of 10 ABC Dec 22 calls, then a short sale of 1,000 shares of ABC stock 4 days later
C) closing sale of 100 shares of ABC stock, then a buy of 1 ABC Dec 22 call 20 days later
D) closing sale of 100 shares of ABC stock, then a short sale 1 ABC Dec 22 put 40 days later

106. A customer invests in a mutual fund with no front-end load and a graduated back-end load that begins at 5% and decreases 1% every year for the first 4 years of investment. No other fees are charged for this mutual fund investment. After 3 years, the net asset value (NAV) has appreciated by 10%, and the customer redeems his entire investment in the mutual fund. If the customer's initial investment was $2 million, how much money does he receive upon exiting the investment?

A) $2,040,000
B) $2,156,000
C) $2,178,000
D) $2,200,000

107. An aggravated customer closes her brokerage account at XYZ Broker Brothers in protest of an unsatisfactory execution price on a market order. How long after the account is closed must XYZ Broker Brothers maintain records relating to the customer's account?

   A) 2 years
   B) 3 years
   C) 6 years
   D) 8 years

108. The content of an investment company's sales literature may include which of the following?

   A) inferences about future returns based on past performance
   B) charts and analysis based only on past performance
   C) commentary about future returns without discussion of risks and limitations
   D) assurances that the fund manager will not lose an investor's money

109. A moderately bearish customer buys a Jan 30/35 QRS put spread for $2.80 when the market price of QRS stock is $33.20. What is the customer's break-even price on this trade?

   A) $32.20
   B) $32.80
   C) $33.20
   D) $33.80

110. At the beginning of the first quarter of a calendar year, a public company has 1,000,000 shares authorized; 500,000 shares outstanding; and 100,000 shares in Treasury. The company announces that it has authorized a buyback of exactly 200,000 shares during the second quarter. Which of the following MOST likely represents the state of its common stock in the upcoming third quarter?

   A) 1,200,000 shares authorized; 500,000 shares outstanding; 300,000 shares in Treasury
   B) 1,000,000 shares authorized; 300,000 shares outstanding; 100,000 shares in Treasury
   C) 1,000,000 shares authorized; 300,000 shares outstanding; 300,000 shares in Treasury
   D) 1,200,000 shares authorized; 300,000 shares outstanding; 300,000 shares in Treasury

111. What is the bond ratio of a public company whose capital structure consists entirely of $20 million in outstanding 6-month commercial paper; $200 million in outstanding 10-year debentures; and an equity market capitalization of $600 million?

   A) 1/30
   B) 1/4
   C) 11/41
   D) 1/3

112. Of the following, which is a federally taxable, federally subsidized municipal bond?

   A) Treasury note
   B) general obligation bond
   C) Revenue Anticipation Note
   D) Build America Bonds

113. PQR Corp., an aircraft manufacturer based in the United States, raises $90 million via a 30-year bond sold exclusively to individual investors outside the United States. PQR Corp. does not register the issuance with the SEC. Which of the following Securities Act safe-harbor provisions is most applicable to this bond?

   A) Regulation S
   B) Rule 144a
   C) Rule 504 of Regulation D
   D) Section 3(a)(2)

114. CDE Textile Corp. has authorized twenty-two million shares of common stock for issuance. Ten million are outstanding, and one million are held in treasury. In the recent quarter, CDE Textile closed the sale of a small textile mill for $11 million and approved a measure to distribute these sale proceeds as a special cash dividend. What amount will be paid to an investor who holds one share of CDE common stock on the record date of this special cash dividend?

   A) $1.10
   B) $1.00
   C) $0.50
   D) $0.33

115. Which of the following can be described as a blank-check company?
    A) unit investment trust company
    B) special purpose acquisition company
    C) direct participation program
    D) Depository Trust & Clearing Corp.

116. What is the maximum potential loss of a VWX Dec 22/11 put credit spread traded at $5.44?
    A) $2,200
    B) $1,100
    C) $556
    D) $456

117. A noninstitutional customer buys a corporate bond on the day of a fixed-price offering at the public offering price from a broker-dealer who acquired the security as part of the offering. Which of the following must be included in the customer's transaction confirmation?
    A) National Best Bid at the time of the transaction
    B) National Best Offer at the time of the transaction
    C) the execution time of the transaction, expressed to the second
    D) the broker's markup, expressed as a dollar amount and percentage

118. A NYSE floor broker receives a limit not-held order from a customer who wants to sell 25,000 shares of PQR stock at $19.90 or better. The National Best Bid and Offer (NBBO) for PQR stock is displayed as $19.85/$19.95. Which of the following orders, if given to the NYSE floor broker by a different customer, could trade against the customer's order as a NYSE 72(d) cross?
    A) limit order to pay $19.85 or better for 25,000 shares of PQR
    B) limit order to pay $19.90 or better for 8,000 shares of PQR
    C) limit order to pay $19.95 or better for 12,500 shares of PQR
    D) limit order to pay $20.10 or better for 9,500 shares of PQR

119. Up to how many years after an alleged violation of FINRA rules may a complaint seeking arbitration be submitted?
    A) 3
    B) 4
    C) 6
    D) 9

120. An options trader owns SPX calls that expire in-the-money. What does she receive upon exercise?
    A) SPX futures contracts
    B) constituent stocks in the S&P 500 Index
    C) shares of the SPY exchange-traded fund
    D) cash

121. A 65-year-old customer who hopes to retire soon wants to invest a quarter of his savings into one of the following packaged products. Which is likely to be the LEAST suitable?
    A) wildcatting DPP
    B) tower REIT
    C) high-dividend-yield ETF
    D) Treasury bill ETF

122. A young professional invests $10,000 in a new issue of a 1-year Treasury security at a yield to maturity of 1%. What is the semiannual coupon payment of this position?
    A) $0
    B) $10
    C) $50
    D) $100

123. Which of the following is exempt from disclosure on the FINRA's BrokerCheck website?
    A) the full name of an associated person
    B) the reason for termination of an associated person as reported by a member on Form U5
    C) registration history of associated persons before their present employment with a member
    D) information about a Final Regulatory Action where an associated person was the subject

124. A salesperson wants to drum up business by sending a letter to retail customers about opportunities presented by a multi-class agency debt instrument backed by a pool of mortgage pass-through securities or mortgage loans. All of the following must be included in this letter, EXCEPT

   A) the term *collateralized mortgage obligation* in the name of the product.
   B) a disclosure that agency backing applies to the product's face value, not to any premium paid.
   C) a comparison between this product and a bank certificate of deposit.
   D) a disclosure that yield will fluctuate with the prepayment rate of the underlying mortgages.

125. An options trader sells 1 XYZ Jan 22 call contract at $3.44. Her brokerage requires her to post $2,500 in margin against this trade. In theory, what is the maximum amount that she can lose on this short call position?

   A) $344
   B) $2,200
   C) $2,500
   D) infinite

126. For a person other than the customer to exercise discretionary power in a particular customer account, a member firm must acquire and document all of the following EXCEPT

   A) written authorization from the customer.
   B) the date discretionary power shall expire.
   C) the date discretionary power is granted.
   D) the signature(s) of the person(s) authorized to exercise discretionary power in the account.

127. Why might a shareholder participate in a rights offering?

   A) a desire to retain proportional ownership in a business
   B) the opportunity to buy equity at a subscription price below the market price for the stock
   C) as a means to provide funds to a company in which the shareholder is already invested
   D) any of the above

128. Who is responsible for rendering a legal opinion upon the validity of a municipal bond issue and the applicability of tax exemptions?

   A) bond counsel
   B) lead underwriter
   C) issuer
   D) conduit borrower

129. An options buyer paid $8.42 for the CDE Jul 44 straddle on March 1. At that time, CDE stock was trading at $43.20. Today, 1 month later, CDE stock continues to trade at $43.20, and the implied volatility of the CDE Jul 44 call remains the same as it was on March 1. CDE is a growth company that does not pay shareholder dividends. Assuming no interest rate effects, what is the CDE Jul 44 straddle worth today?

   A) more than $8.42
   B) equal to $8.42
   C) less than $8.42
   D) not enough information

130. Which of the following explains why asset-backed securities (ABSs) often trade at a higher yield than corporate bullet bonds of the same maturity?

   A) Issuers of ABS tend to have worse credit quality than corporate issuers.
   B) Bullet bonds are guaranteed against default; ABS lacks this guarantee.
   C) Investors seek to be compensated for ABS prepayment risk.
   D) ABS is a new and small market in comparison to corporate bullet bonds.

131. The bid for the GHIJ Dec 40 call is $1.40, and the option is offered at $1.50. The bid for the GHIJ Dec 45 call is $0.10, and the option is offered at $0.40. Based on these displayed quotations, at what price is the GHIJ Dec 40/45 bull call spread offered?

   A) $1.00
   B) $1.40
   C) $1.50
   D) $1.90

132. A FINRA member sells software that enables investors to perform analysis of various securities. This software (and any related retail communications) must

  A) come with a written disclosure of its limitations and assumptions.
  B) be fully functional with all securities in the selected asset class.
  C) reflect actual future investment results.
  D) provide the same results consistently when used repeatedly.

133. When can a registered principal supervise their own activities?

  A) never
  B) only on principal transactions
  C) only on agency transactions
  D) only when unavoidable

134. Upon the ex-dividend date for a large special cash dividend payable to shareholders by QRS Computer Corp., the share price of QRS stock reduces by the amount of the dividend. How does this affect call option contracts?

  A) Call options lose value due to large special cash dividends.
  B) Call options appreciate due to large special cash dividends.
  C) Call options are subject to strike adjustment by the amount of a large special dividend.
  D) Call options are unaffected by special cash dividends.

135. A customer purchases a new-issue municipal bond at $96, which matures in 20 years. He sells the bond after 8 years at $92. What is the gain or loss on the sale?

  A) $76 gain
  B) $80 gain
  C) $40 loss
  D) $56 loss

Answer Key

1. **C)** FINRA Rule 2210 sets certain requirements for approval, review, and record-keeping of institutional communications, and establishes a different standard for institutional communications than for retail communications. In general, the institutional standards are looser because of the greater level of awareness and sophistication expected of securities professionals. Option C correctly interprets subsection 2210(a)(4), which states, "No member may treat a communication as having been distributed to an institutional investor if the member has reason to believe that the communication or any excerpt thereof will be forwarded or made available to any retail investor."

2. **A)** The investor sold a put to collect a $300 credit. (US-listed single-name equity options carry a 100 multiplier.) The put contract carried a $200 intrinsic value upon expiry, which counts as a loss against the initial $300 credit for a net $100 gain on the contract. The initial spot price of LMNO stock and the fact that $48 is the all-time low are not relevant. The breakeven, or zero profit-and-loss point, for this options trade was $47.

3. **A)** Zero-coupon bonds are among the most straightforward debt products because they comprise only one cash flow. When yield is above zero, a zero-coupon bond trades at a discount because the investor's only profit comes from the difference between the initial price and the cash flow upon maturity.

4. **C)** Current yield equals annual coupon income divided by the bond's market price. This simple calculation reflects the rate of annual cash flow generated by purchasing the bond. In other words, current yield is the annual return on investment stemming solely from the bond's periodic income. The annual coupon is 7.00%, and the face value is $10,000, so the bond's annual coupon amounts to $700. Dividing the coupon by the market price of $14,000 results in a current yield of 5.00%.

5. **C)** In-the-money call options should sometimes be exercised before an ex-dividend date because their time value (premium minus intrinsic) may be less than the amount of the dividend. Use this fact to solve the question by process of elimination. Option D can be eliminated immediately because only the long holder can choose to early exercise an option. Option A can also be eliminated because put options do not need to be early exercised due to ex-dividend dates. (There are other rare cases where puts should be early exercised.) Not only does the Oct 60 call in Option B have more time value than the Jul 30 call in Option C (because it is longer-dated and closer to at-the-money); it is also an out-of-the-money option because TUV stock is trading at $55.00. It would not be smart to pay $60.00 for a stock that can be bought in the open market for $55.00, so Option B can be eliminated.

    This leaves Option C, a long Jul 30 call that is both deeply in-the-money and shorter dated than the Oct 60 call. In the context of an upcoming dividend, the investor would be wise to review this Jul 30 call in her portfolio and consider early exercise. Upon reviewing this contract, the investor may find that its time value exceeds $0.20 and choose to forgo early exercise, or she may find that its time value is lesser, and that early exercise is the wiser decision.

6. **D)** Inflation-linked bonds, or "linkers," are used by bondholders who want to protect their investments from the effects of devaluing currency. The US Treasury established a

government-issued linker, Treasury Inflation-Protected Securities (TIPS), in 1997. TIPS are available in 5-year, 10-year, and 30-year maturities. TIPS are more expensive than a conventional bond but offer the added protection of principal adjustment based on the Consumer Price Index (CPI). Mortgage-Backed Securities (MBSs), Separate Trading of Registered Interest and Principal of Securities (STRIPS), and Treasury Investment Growth Receipts (TIGRs) are not linked to the rate of inflation.

7. **B)** A sinking fund allows a bond issuer to smoothly retire debt, often by buying it in the secondary market. The issuer's secondary market activity contributes to liquidity and provides an ever-present bid that can stabilize the market by supporting the bond's price in periods of volatility. However, an investor would not be so keen on an optional acceleration feature, whereby the issuer can retire the debt faster than expected. This is similar to a call provision, but the optional acceleration feature allows debt to be retired at the sinking fund price, whereas a call price is typically higher.

8. **B)** Municipal Securities Rulemaking Board (MSRB) Rule G-21 defines a product advertisement as "any advertisement concerning one or more specific municipal securities, one or more specific issues of municipal securities, the municipal securities of one or more specific issuers, or the specific features of municipal securities." Each such advertisement must be approved by a general securities principal or municipal securities principal (a person registered to be a manager) before the advertisement's first use.

9. **A)** Prior to approval of the registration statement for a securities offering (like an IPO), the preliminary prospectus carries a red disclaimer that states the offering remains unapproved and cannot be bid on nor offered until approval takes place. This red disclaimer is the source of the nickname red herring for a preliminary prospectus awaiting Securities and Exchange Commission (SEC) approval.

10. **D)** According to FINRA, a pattern day trader is any margin customer who executes four or more day trades during a 5-business-day period if those day trades constitute more than 6% of the trader's total activity during the same time frame. A pattern day trader must maintain equity of $25,000 or more in the margin account in order to day-trade.

11. **D)** There are several red flags in this transaction. The customer generally trades bank stocks and her foray into the commodity markets is questionable, but a single large exchange-traded fund (ETF) trade alone is not necessarily inconsistent with the customer's trading strategy. However, the fact that she wants to trade the opposite direction at the same price demonstrates a clear lack of regard for transaction costs and commissions. Furthermore, the time frame of the trades is very fast, and there is no clear profit motive involved. Finally, using two different accounts for trading activity with a net-zero risk position is strange because it cannot be part of an overall profit-seeking strategy for the customer's firm. In compliance with FINRA Rule 3310, every broker-dealer is required to look for signs of suspicious activity that may suggest money laundering. When a red flag is observed, the broker-dealer ought to perform additional due diligence before proceeding with the transaction, as in Option D.

12. **D)** Municipal securities regulations exempt some offerings from the SEC Rule 15c2-12 disclosure requirement to prepare an official statement. These exemptions include offerings smaller than $1 million, offerings with minimum denominations (unit size) of $100,000 sold to thirty-five or fewer "sophisticated" investors, and offerings with minimum denominations of $100,000 that mature in 9 months or less from their date of issuance.

Option A is exempt due to its small size, below $1 million. Option B is exempt due to its large denominations as well as the small number and sophistication of its investors. Option C is exempt due to its very near-dated maturity. Option D does not meet the "$100,000 minimum denomination" condition, and its size is much larger than $1 million, so it does not meet the criteria for exemption from the preparation of an official statement.

13. **B)** These two bonds are identical except for the call provision, so the question asks how a call provision affects the value of a bond. A

call provision permits the issuer to repay debt early by delivering the redemption price (in this case, equal to face value) to the bondholder. It is a form of optionality granted to the issuer; if interest rates fall, the issuer can borrow money elsewhere at a lower rate to refinance the existing callable bond. The same cannot be done with a noncallable bond that pays coupons until maturity. Thus, the callable bond uniquely exposes its investor to redemption risk in scenarios where rates fall, and it should be priced strictly lower than its noncallable equivalent. Adding a callable provision never increases the value of an interest-bearing bond.

14. **D)** A strangle is an option strategy made up of a call and a put of the same maturity, both traded in the same direction, with the put having a lower strike price than the call. Option A is incorrect because the investor needs to buy a put to establish a strangle using the call he currently owns. Option B is wrong too; purchasing a Sep 38 put establishes a straddle because both legs of the strategy share the 38 strike. Option C is incorrect because the Aug 36 put does not share a maturity with the investor's existing Sep 38 call. The remaining option—a Sep 36 put—would establish the GHIJ Sep 36/38 strangle, so Option D is correct.

15. **C)** Double-barreled bonds are municipal bonds that use revenue to pay debt service and back that revenue with a general obligation (GO) bond on the part of the issuer. They offer two levels of security to the bondholder.

16. **A)** FINRA Rule 2111 establishes a suitability standard for investment recommendations. This rule does not strictly define suitability but suggests that "a customer's investment profile includes, but is not limited to, the customer's age, other investments, financial situation and needs, tax status, investment objectives, investment experience, investment time horizon, liquidity needs, risk tolerance, and any other information the customer may disclose." Suitability is not a conditional standard, and a registered representative must make suitable recommendations (or none at all) whether the customer is expected to act on them or not. This means Option A is correct. Option B describes a customer's liquidity needs, Option C describes a customer's time horizon, and Option D describes a customer's risk tolerance. All three must be considered by the broker according to FINRA Rule 2111.

17. **A)** A pass-through mortgage-backed security (MBS) takes the income from a pool of mortgages and distributes it among holders of the security. In contrast, a collateralized mortgage obligation (CMO) distributes that mortgage income according to tranches. CMO products will have a different risk profile from pass-through MBS products even when the underlying pool of mortgages is identical because the two products divide mortgage cash flows differently. A collateralized debt obligation (CDO) works similarly to a CMO but can include other forms of debt contracts (not just mortgages). Asset-backed securities (ABS) do not include residential mortgages, but they can include home equity loans and other personal debt (like credit card receivables).

18. **D)** Current yield equals the annual income divided by the market value. Assume that only the definition of current yield is known. To solve this problem the long way, convert from the current yield to the market value, reduce the market value by 20.0% to account for the price action in the market, and then convert back into current yield terms. If the current yield was initially 4.0% and the annual income is 8.0%, then the price must be $200 to begin with. A 20.0% reduction in market price leaves the bond at $160, which leaves a new current yield of 8/160 = 5.0%.

    There is also a shortcut. Because yields and prices move inversely, a 20.0% reduction in price should cause yield to increase. The exact amount of this increase can be determined using algebra. Because the coupon rate doesn't change, the initial current yield can be divided by (1 - 20.0%) = 0.8 to find the new current yield. Indeed, 4.0% divided by 0.8 equals 5.0% (0.04 ÷ 0.8 = 0.05).

19. **C)** A registered representative may not trade stock for her firm's benefit ahead of a customer's market order for the same stock in the same direction. This is front-running, and it harms the customer by both impacting the market price ahead of the customer execution and delaying the customer's market access. Whether the registered representative has already begun the

process of placing (or thinking about placing) an order is irrelevant. Front-running is unlawful, and it violates several regulations including FINRA Rules 2010, 5270, 5310, and 5320.

20. **B)** A stock's dividend yield is equal to its annual dividend income divided by its market price. In the case of VWXY, the annual dividend income is $1.20 because investors receive four $0.30 dividends every year, per share held. This figure divided by the last trade price of $24.00 is equal to 5.00%.

    Note the similarity between the dividend yield of a stock and the current yield of a bond. Both are computed by dividing the annual income distributions by the market price of the security.

21. **A)** This a discretionary account: the customer has already signed documents giving written permission for the broker to effect trades of reasonable and appropriate size, frequency, and character. Because this is a discretionary account, the registered representative is authorized to trade without specific instructions from the customer. If the account were nondiscretionary, the registered representative would require a verbal instruction for the specific trade or a written authorization for discretionary trading in accordance with FINRA Rule 3260.

22. **B)** Gifts to an individual with a value that is less than the annual gift tax exclusion, $15,000 in 2021, are not taxable. If the gifts exceed this gift tax exclusion, they are taxable for the giver. The tax rate for the taxable gift would be 0% until the giver's lifetime gift tax exemption has been exhausted. The receiver of the gift is not taxed in any of these cases.

23. **C)** FINRA Rule 2231 clarifies that, barring certain exceptions that require customer consent in writing or special exemptions by FINRA itself, account statements must be issued at least quarterly.

24. **C)** The first transaction created 700 contracts; it was an opening transaction for both counterparties. The second transaction passed 500 of those contracts to a different institution without creating or eliminating any contracts. Thus, at the start of business on Thursday, there exist 700 contracts in the marketplace, all of which were created in the initial transaction. Open interest counts the total number of extant contracts in the marketplace. It does not reflect the aggregate volume of contracts traded.

25. **D)** FINRA maintains records of the associated persons registered at its member firms and requires Form U5 to be filed by member firms within 30 days of a registered representative's termination.

26. **C)** A balloon mortgage involves lump-sum repayment of some or all of the principal upon maturity. That is not generally the case with the other options, whereby interest and principal will be paid throughout the life of the contract. Another example of a non-amortizing asset is a credit card: the cardholder can make minimum payments into perpetuity and continue to saturate the line of credit.

27. **A)** The customer's trade costs $16,000 total. When PQRS stock fell from $800 to $400, it wiped out the equivalent of half of the position's value ($8,000) from the customer's equity, leaving $1,000 in equity. The position's remaining value of $8,000 requires a minimum margin of 25%, or $2,000. The customer must deposit $1,000 in additional margin to maintain the position per FINRA Rule 4210.

28. **B)** To compute the profit or loss of the options trade held to expiry, determine the initial cost of the trade and the final intrinsic value. To find the initial cost of the trade, remember that twenty contracts were purchased for $450 each (incorporating the 100 multiplier), for a total debit of $9,000. The final intrinsic value is a bit more complicated. The stock appreciates by 10% of its initial price, or $5.20, and closes at $57.20 on Sep expiration. Subtracting $55.00 (the strike price of the call option) from $57.20 to get an intrinsic value of $2.20 ($57.20 - $55.00 = $2.20). This amounts to a final value of $4,400 (20 × $2.20 = 44; incorporating the 100 multiplier: $4,400). The customer started with $9,000 and ended with $4,400, so he lost $4,600 ($9,000 - $4,400 = $4,600).

29. **C)** There is no reason to believe that this bond is backed by a specific pool of equipment, assets, or cash flows, so Options A and D can

be eliminated. The bond is callable after 3 years, so STUV Industries could refund the bond by borrowing at a lower rate elsewhere in order to retire this bond early. That eliminates Option B. This bond is a step-up bond (Option C) because its annual coupon income eventually increases over time. A step-up bond may also be called a stairway bond.

30. **C)** Some account holdings cannot change hands via the Automated Customer Account Transfer Service (ACATS). Among these are securities sold exclusively by the old firm, mutual and money market funds not available at the new firm, bankrupt securities, privately placed limited partnerships, and annuities. When a particular security cannot be transferred via ACATS, it can either remain at the old brokerage or be liquidated for cash. (In some cases, the customer can also take possession of the security.)

31. **C)** Beta is a measure of the historically determined sensitivity of the change in the price of an asset (here, FGH) with respect to the change in another market variable (in this case, SPX). A strongly negative correlation means that the return of SPX can be multiplied by the given beta to make a reasonable guess at the performance of FGH. Negative 2% × -1.5 equals positive 3% (-0.02 × -1.5 = 0.03). If a $100 asset appreciates by 3%, then its final price is $103.

32. **D)** The price-to-earnings (P/E) ratio tells how much the company earns annually relative to its equity price. DEF makes a consistent profit, so it is not necessary to consider the trailing 12-month profit, predict future 12-month profits, or quadruple the most recent quarterly profit—all paths suggest an annual profit of $1.40 per share. Dividing the share price by this annual earnings-per-share figure computes a P/E ratio of 50.

33. **A)** In general, interest expenses for personal consumer debt (like credit cards and auto loans) are not tax-deductible; however, corporations may deduct interest expenses for debt service. One example of this is a corporation's tax deduction of a bond coupon payment.

34. **C)** In the United States, the convention for corporate bond interest accrual is "30/360."

Every month comprises 30 days, and every year consists of 360 days. With 30/360 accrual, February (or any other complete month) accrues a twelfth of the annual coupon income, and each individual day would be considered to accrue 1/360 of the annual coupon income.

35. **B)** This strategy is a call butterfly. Its maximum payout is half of its width minus the premium paid, and its maximum loss is the premium paid. Like a straddle or a strangle, a butterfly is a symmetrical strategy. One of its break-even points is the lowest strike plus the premium paid. The other is the highest strike minus the premium paid.

    The net premium paid for this long butterfly is a total debit of $3.40 for the wings, minus a total credit of $2.40 for the guts. That amounts to a $1 debit ($3.40 - $2.40 = $1.00). The given breakeven is $1.00 less than the highest strike ($40.00), so the remaining breakeven must be $1.00 more than the lowest strike ($30.00), which comes to $31.00.

36. **B)** The buying price equals the public offering price (POP), given as $10.00/share. The selling price equals the net asset value (NAV), computed as $9.50/share by subtracting the sales charge (SC) from the POP ($10.00 - $0.50 = $9.50). In this case, the SC is exactly 5% of the POP, so the recouped amount upon liquidation is $950,000. The management expense ratio (MER) is not charged directly to the investor but is instead drawn out of the NAV. If the NAV has not changed over the course of the year, it means that the fees, expenses, and taxes of the mutual fund have been exactly equal to its returns.

37. **D)** Alternative trading systems (ATSs) (for example, a dark pool) are not exchanges, but each ATS is required to report the trades that cross on its platform. This information must be delivered to a FINRA Trade Reporting Facility (TRF) within 10 seconds. The Trade Reporting and Compliance System (TRACE) performs a similar function for the over-the-counter (OTC) fixed-income securities market and requires reporting as soon as practicable within 15 minutes.

38. **C)** This provision is a put because it accelerates the payout at the election of the bondholder, typically when interest rates rise, and the bondholder wants to reinvest the principal elsewhere at a higher rate. A soft put permits the issuer to deliver the accelerated payout in the form of common stock, other bonds, preferred stock, or perhaps other securities. The issuer here delivered common stock, so the put must be a soft put.

39. **D)** To be considered an accredited investor, a person must hold an active Series 7, Series 65, or Series 82 license. Alternatively, a person with a net worth exceeding $1 million (excluding the primary residence, with some penalties for underwater mortgage debt or recent home equity loans), either alone or with a spouse, is also considered an accredited investor. Finally, a person who expects to earn $200,000 or more annually and has earned the same for the past 2 years ($300,000 if considered jointly with a spouse) is also considered an accredited investor. Additional criteria exist for trusts and other entities, but these are the criteria for natural persons. Option A meets the net worth test. Option B meets the licensing test. Option C meets the income test (jointly with spouse). Option D fails all of the tests unless the engineer happens to be a registered representative.

40. **B)** Delivery versus payment is either triggered by payment or implemented to transact simultaneously, so Option B is correct. The purpose of delivery versus payment is to minimize settlement-related counterparty risk by quickly executing both sides of the transaction after both have been guaranteed. Delivery versus free is incorrect because, in this method, delivery is made before payment with no guarantee of immediacy; payment may occur on a different business day. Cash settlement is incorrect because no physical security changes hands in this method. Delivery versus delivery is incorrect because, despite meeting the immediacy requirement, this method exchanges physical for physical.

41. **B)** The date of record is the point at which a snapshot of the stockholder's roster is taken for the purpose of paying out the dividend. A trade must settle on or before the date of record for the buyer to collect the dividend. GHI stock, like all US-listed stocks, settles on a T + 2 cycle. If the date of record falls on Thursday, then the last day a buyer can expect to receive the dividend is Tuesday. On Wednesday, the stock begins to trade ex-dividend (without the dividend).

42. **C)** FINRA Rule 4513 permits one of two methods of storing written customer complaints at the supervisory office of a member firm that corresponds to the complaint. The member firm is permitted to aggregate all complaints and store them together, or to maintain a separate register of those complaints and where to find them in the office's archives. Regardless of the record-keeping method, the complaint and the action taken by the member firm must be preserved for a minimum of 4 years.

43. **A)** A warrant is an option. It is a source of equity financing for a corporation because those holders who decide to exercise their warrants pay the company in exchange for equity. Warrants have some major differences from listed call options insofar as they do not face a clearinghouse, they tend to be very long-dated, and they can be written with nonstandard terms (or even structured as puts). Also, the issuance and exercise of warrants affect the company's bottom line and can dilute shareholder equity. Still, given the suggested tools, an option pricing tool is clearly the most practical.

44. **B)** An immediate-or-cancel (IOC) order differs from a fill-or-kill (FOK) order in only one way: an IOC order permits partial fills, while an FOK order does not. From the perspective of the IOC order, any available liquidity will be absorbed, and any leftover piece of the order will be canceled. From the perspective of the FOK order, if the total amount of desired liquidity is available, the order will transact; otherwise, the entire order will be canceled. In this case, the FOK order gets filled completely, and the IOC order gets filled partially in the amount corresponding to the size of the FOK order.

45. **A)** The Real-Time Transaction Reporting System (RTRS) is administered by the Municipal Securities Rulemaking Board (MSRB). It performs a similar price-discovery function to the Trade Reporting and Compliance System (TRACE), and both of these trade reporting systems have a 15-minute reporting requirement

from the time of trade. RTRS shows trades between dealers as well as customer trades.

46. **C)** Since the maximum aggregate annual Coverdell ESA contribution for a single beneficiary is $2,000 (not including rollovers from certain other Coverdell ESA accounts), the most this customer can contribute is $1,500 because the beneficiary's mother already contributed $500 ($2,000 − $500 = $1,500).

47. **A)** The operant difference between Roth and traditional IRAs is that traditional accounts are funded with pretax contributions and taxed upon withdrawal during retirement, while Roth accounts are funded with posttax contributions and not taxed upon withdrawal during retirement. The customer's income profile, lifestyle, and retirement plans clearly indicate that contributions will be made in years when his taxable income is far higher, so there is likely to be a tax benefit accrued by using a traditional IRA and paying tax in retirement rather than at the time of contribution.

48. **A)** This approach is known as dollar-cost averaging. Resist the urge to assume that the customer's average share price is $30.00 simply because that is the mean of the three prices stated. Remember that the customer bought more shares of WXYZ at the lower price than at the higher prices. In fact, she bought sixty shares for $15.00, thirty shares for $30.00, and only twenty shares for $45.00. The customer purchased 110 shares with a total of $2,700, amounting to an average price of $24.55.

49. **D)** The market for penny stocks has historically been marked by highly speculative trades. Low liquidity and a low barrier to entry make this market a target for high-pressure sales tactics and predatory behavior. Rule 15g-2 of the Securities Exchange Act of 1934 aims to illuminate the risks presented by penny stocks and the market in which they are transacted by requiring customers to acknowledge in writing that they have received a document disclosing those risks before their first trade of a penny stock.

50. **B)** The bond is offered at its clean price. To know its dirty price, compute and add the accrued interest. Accrual for a US corporate bond is computed according to a 30/360 convention. November and December count for 30 days each, and there are 12 additional days, for a total of 72 days of accrual. 72/360 simplifies to 1/5, which means that 20% of the annual coupon income of $120 (12% × $1,000) has accrued. The dirty price is $1,754, equal to an accrual of $24 plus the clean price of $1,730.

51. **D)** In general, Regulation SHO requires borrow to be located before shares can be sold short (as would be the case here). However, there is an exception to this requirement: a market maker engaging in bona fide market-making activity is permitted to sell shares short without having located borrow before effecting the short sale.

52. **B)** A New York Stock Exchange (NYSE) market-on-close or limit-on-close order allows the trader to participate in the closing auction for MNO stock, which prints at one single price no matter how many orders are involved. Because of its liquidity and price transparency, the NYSE closing auction is often used as a reference price for equity derivatives and other securities. The NYSE closing auction features auction price collars. A stock that is priced above $50.00, like MNO, cannot move by more than 1% on the closing auction. Stocks priced between $25.01 and $50.00 cannot move by more than 2%. Stocks priced at $25.00 or less cannot move by more than 5% unless the move is $0.15 or smaller. In this way, the NYSE market-on-close order provides some guarantees against unexpected price dislocation.

53. **D)** The customer's transaction pattern is not particularly speculative because it actually reduces his exposure to stock price movements. It is not arbitrage because only one transaction is effected at a time, and no relative price discrepancy is being sought or collected. The transaction may be a hedge, but it is not a particularly effective one because it does not buy the customer any exposure to increased volatility and leaves him exposed to downside risk for UVW stock. It is clearly a yield enhancement because the customer—in addition to dividends and long-term capital gains from UVW itself—is collecting premium by selling fully hedged call options. Option D is therefore correct.

This strategy is commonly called an overwrite because a call option is written over a stock position that matches or exceeds it in size. It is a common practice among asset managers who are in search of increased yield from their equity positions.

54. **B)** Rule 144A of the Securities Act of 1933 establishes that certain private placement offerings that are unregistered with the SEC may be traded only by qualified institutional buyers (QIBs). Rule 144A is a safe harbor from registration requirements. It can be viewed as a stepping-stone to the more rigorous process of raising capital via an initial public offering (IPO). The most obvious limitation of a Rule 144A security is that QIBs are usually institutional investors who manage over $100 million. This is a higher standard than the one used to determine whether a person or entity is an accredited investor.

55. **A)** American depositary receipts (ADRs) are domestically listed securities, denominated in dollars, that represent a stake in a foreign company's equity. Unfortunately for ADR investors, their dividends are often taxed in both the foreign country and the United States. Option A is correct because ADRs are never denominated in foreign currencies.

56. **D)** Among other requirements, real estate investment trusts (REITs) are typically required to generate at least 75% of their income from real property or debt thereof. A construction loan, a network tower rent, and a collateralized mortgage obligation (CMO) all generate income from real property. An auto loan, however, generates income from personal property and could never serve as the core cash stream of a real estate investment trust.

57. **A)** When investors buy a calendar spread, they buy a longer-dated call and sell a shorter-dated call against it. The shorter-dated call is cheaper because it has less time value; the spread costs a net debit when traded in this direction. Parity is another word for intrinsic value, so liquidating a position "for parity when WXY trades $28.00" means that the investor sold the option for its intrinsic value versus $28.00 in the underlier.

To answer the question, decompose this trade into three transactions: 1) the investor paid $2.20 for 1 long WXY Feb 25 call and 1 short WXY Jan 25 call; 2) the WXY Jan 25 call expired out-of-the-money (worthless); 3) the WXY Feb 25 call was liquidated for a credit of $3.00. This amounts to $0.80, or $80.00, when factoring in the 100 contract multiplier for listed stock options.

58. **C)** FINRA Rule 5220 prohibits the bond trader from backing away from a firm offer. Since the bond trader did not contact either customer to revise his quotation, he is obligated to transact with each of them at the specified price and size. There is no justification to revise the offer for Customer B; in some markets, prices can change wildly within the span of 5 minutes, but that is generally not the case for a 30-year corporate bond.

59. **C)** Terms like *resistance* are part of the jargon of technical analysis. This is a controversial topic among traders, but every registered representative should be familiar with the terms that technical analysts use to communicate about price movements. Resistance describes selling pressure that impedes a rallying price, and the term support describes buying pressure that similarly impedes a sell-off. A stock that is "consolidating" is trading within a fixed range bounded by support on the downside and resistance on the upside. A "breakout" occurs when the price decisively crosses a historical or perceived resistance or support level. A stock that is "overbought" is believed to be due for a reversion downward because its price appreciation has exceeded a level considered to be its intrinsic value. (A stock described as "oversold" is due for a reversion upward for a similar reason.) This question could be rephrased as a statement: "When the price of stock TUVW increases toward $70, more sellers enter the market and cause the stock price to decrease again." You may encounter technical jargon on the Series 7 exam and should therefore spend some time familiarizing yourself with it.

60. **A)** All of these corporations issue debt that is backed by loans or loan derivatives. Ginnie Mae is the Government National Mortgage Association (GNMA), and the debt that it issues is guaranteed by the full faith and credit of the US government, just like Treasury bonds.

Freddie Mac is the Federal Home Loan Mortgage Corporation. Farmer Mac is the Federal Agricultural Mortgage Corporation. Fannie Mae is the Federal National Mortgage Association. All three of these companies are known as government-sponsored enterprises (GSEs). They were created by Congress to foster public purposes, but they are shareholder-owned corporations. Freddie Mac and Fannie Mae stabilize and support the residential mortgage market, and Farmer Mac serves a similar purpose in the markets for rural housing and agricultural real estate.

61. **A)** When a US-listed stock option is bought or sold, it settles 1 day after the trade date (T + 1). When a US-listed share of stock is bought or sold, it settles 2 days after the trade date (T + 2). The first transaction is a purchase of a call option, so it settles T + 1 (on Tuesday). The second transaction is a purchase of shares between counterparties of the call option, so it settles T + 2 (on Thursday). The third transaction is a sale of stock, so it too settles T + 2 (on Monday of the following week).

62. **C)** FINRA Rule 3220 sets a $100 limit for the total value of annual gifts and gratuities that are given by a FINRA member to an individual with whom the member conducts business.

63. **B)** An equipment trust certificate (ETC) is a debt instrument that is secured by equipment. It was originally used to fund the acquisition of railroad cars, but in modern times ETC financing is frequently used to finance aircraft acquisitions. When used in this way, the ETC does not transfer ownership of the aircraft to the airline until the debt matures. As a result, the aircraft is shielded from any immediate claim by general creditors in the event of bankruptcy. Collateralized mortgage obligations (CMOs) and real estate investment trusts (REITs) refer to securities that are based on real assets, not equipment. DAL is the ticker symbol for the equity of an airline, not a debt security.

64. **A)** An authorized participant can create shares of an exchange-traded fund (ETF)—in this case, SPY—by assembling the proper quantities of the constituent assets and delivering them to the ETF sponsor in exchange for the appropriate number of shares of the ETF. (Net exposure remains the same.) The technical term for this is *creation*. A redemption is the opposite transaction, whereby an authorized participant delivers ETF shares to the ETF sponsor and receives the constituent assets. A reverse conversion is an options trade in which the trader sells stock and puts, and buys calls. A tender offer is a public bid for shareholders to sell their stock.

65. **D)** Discrepancies are bound to arise from time to time in a large marketplace, and the proper response when a trade is unfamiliar and cannot be reconciled as ascribed is DK, or "don't know."

66. **C)** The US Securities and Exchange Commission (SEC) enforces a "quiet period" surrounding certain important dates, including initial public offering (IPO) dates. In the interest of maintaining an orderly market and allowing all investors equal access to material information, a company's executives and agents may not share new information about the company for 40 days after the IPO.

67. **B)** The Options Clearing Corp. (OCC) maintains a document titled "Characteristics and Risks of Standardized Options," often called the options disclosure document (ODD). It is more than 180 pages and must be provided to customers before they buy or sell an option contract. The ODD explains the risks and attributes of listed options. It is available for download, and printed copies are sold at a low price by the OCC.

68. **D)** A firm-commitment underwriting guarantees the issuer that its offering will be fully subscribed. If the underwriters of a firm-commitment initial public offering (IPO) fail to sell the entire issue, they are on the hook to buy the remaining shares. This constitutes an additional risk on the part of the underwriters. An IPO can also be underwritten on a best-efforts basis (where the issuing company has no guarantee that its offering will be fully subscribed) or on an all-or-none basis (where the offering is either sold entirely or canceled).

69. **C)** The put/call volume ratio simply describes the proportion of put options to call options traded in the market during a given time frame. (Similarly, the put/call open interest ratio describes the proportion of put options to call

options outstanding in the market.) An elevated put/call ratio is often construed as an indicator of bearishness in the market; however, this ratio does not describe the full context of the trades made in a given time frame. For example, if a trader sells cash-secured puts on TUVW stock, that transaction will increase the put/call ratio, but it is in fact a bullish trade. The only safe conclusion that can be drawn from the put/call volume ratio is the proportion of option transactions (or, if computed using open interest, the proportion of outstanding contracts) in the market.

70. **A)** An early retirement plan distribution would normally be subject to mandatory 20% withholding, and an early IRA distribution would normally be subject to mandatory 10% withholding. However, when the retirement plan distribution is transacted directly into the IRA (as is the case with a trustee-to-trustee transfer or with a distribution check made out to the IRA), the IRS stipulates that no taxes will be withheld.

71. **D)** Investment-grade bonds are typically quoted in terms of yield rather than price. These yield quotes are represented as a spread to a benchmark security of similar maturity, like a Treasury bond. If the Treasury bond is trading at a yield to maturity of 3.00% and the investment-grade bond is offered at 74 bps, that means the bond's yield to maturity is offered at 3.74%. Price and yield have an inverse relationship, so the lowest price (the best offer) corresponds to the highest yield spread. In other words, the cheaper that you buy a bond, the greater its yield to maturity will be. From a buyer's perspective, the best offer is the one with the highest yield spread.

72. **B)** During the waiting period, also known as the "cooling-off" period, the issuer may not engage in sales activity, but soliciting and receiving nonbinding indications of interest is permitted. This sometimes helps determine demand for the new issue; however, no new information that is not included in the preliminary prospectus may be provided in the process. Also, no deposits may be accepted during the cooling-off period for the purpose of transacting the security after the cooling-off period has ended.

73. **C)** FGH's liquidation produced $110 million that must be divided among the claimants. The company first tries to repay its bondholders, then distributes the remaining proceeds to its shareholders. In the case of a zero-coupon bond (ZCB), the holders are owed their original investment plus the accrued interest, not the full face value. They recoup their original investment of $80 plus the accrued interest of $15 for a total of $95. On a total face value of $100 million, the ZCB holders collect a total of $95 million. Subtracting $95 million in bondholder payments from the original $110 million liquidation proceeds, FGH is left with $15 million to distribute to the holders of common stock. Each share receives $15 because there are one million shares outstanding.

74. **B)** The US Treasury currently issues Treasury notes in terms of 2, 3, 5, 7, and 10 years. Treasury notes bear coupon interest semiannually until maturity. Longer-term Treasury debt is known as a bond rather than a note and bears coupon interest semiannually as well. Shorter-term Treasury debt is known as a bill and does not bear coupon interest.

75. **B)** Because the common stock is settling regular way, the settlement is T + 2 (trade date plus 2 business days).

76. **D)** When a Treasury security trades before its auction, it is traded on a when-issued basis. Unlike front-running and gun-jumping, this is a lawful practice that assists with price discovery and helps Bank G gauge customer demand for the Treasury note. Those who buy a Treasury note on a when-issued basis are entitled to all of the rights and privileges afforded to holders of the security once it is issued.

77. **A)** *Exercise by exception* is the term used by the Options Clearing Corp. (OCC) for its practice of automatically exercising contracts that expire in-the-money by $0.01 or more. If a member firm wants to override this automatic decision (for options that the member holds long), it must advise the OCC before 5:30 p.m. on the day of that option's expiry. In this case, exercise-by-exception processing would not exercise the fifty calls because, at $50, the spot price of BCD is below $50.01 upon the day of expiry. As a result, the options expire worthless, and the

hedge of one million short shares remains. The member firm carries 50 million dollars' worth of short stock through the weekend.

78. **C)** Even when a FINRA member does not itself execute the orders of its customers, its obligation to provide best execution for those orders remains. That obligation cannot be transferred. A member firm that does not conduct an order-by-order review of the execution quality of such an arrangement is required to periodically conduct a regular and rigorous review at least quarterly.

79. **C)** The customer's order was correctly executed but incorrectly reported, so the customer will be filled at the execution price of $5.40 rather than the initially reported price of $5.30. Despite this error in communicating the execution price, the customer must accept the execution as actually transacted.

80. **D)** For every account held by a customer who is a natural person, FINRA requires that members keep records of the customer's name and residence. In addition, the customer's legal age status must be known, and if the customer is under eighteen, the contact information for a trusted guardian of that individual must also be kept. The member must also keep track of any associated persons assigned to monitor or interact with the account, as well as the signature of a principal denoting that the account was opened in accordance with the firm's policies and procedures. For noninstitutional accounts in which investments go beyond the scope of mutual fund shares not recommended by the member or the member's associated persons, a FINRA member is required to make a reasonable effort to obtain the customer's social security number, occupation, employer address, and status as an associated person of another firm. This effort must be made before settlement of the first transaction in the account.

81. **C)** An income bond only promises coupon payments when the issuer earns sufficient profits to cover them. Similarly, a revenue bond only promises coupon payments when the public project that it finances generates income. Cumulative preferred stockholders accrue unpaid distributions for future payment.

However, regardless of its place in the capital structure, a subordinated debenture carries an obligation to fund debt service; failure to do so is a default.

82. **A)** Option prices are directly based on expected (implied) volatility. In fact, options are often called vol by those who trade them. It is not necessary to know specific options math computations for the Series 7 exam, but it is important to know that, in a general sense, option prices are based on expectations of volatility. When expected volatility increases, option prices go up as well. This question asks how expected volatility affects the price of a 3-month at-the-money (ATM) straddle. Comparing like for like, an ATM straddle costs more when greater volatility is expected over its lifetime.

83. **C)** Intrastate offerings are exempt from SEC registration under a safe-harbor provision of Rule 147 of the Securities Act of 1933. To qualify, the issuer must be incorporated in the state of distribution, must conduct a large amount of its business there, and the securities must be offered and sold exclusively to residents of that state.

84. **A)** Current yield is the ratio of annual coupon income to market price, and nominal yield is the ratio of annual coupon income to face value. For par bonds, the current yield equals the nominal yield because the bond's coupon rate matches the interest rate demanded by the market. Original issue Treasury bonds are par bonds because they are purchased at face value with the coupon rate set by auction. Discount bonds trade below their face value, which means their current yield is greater than their nominal yield. Premium bonds trade above their face value, so their current yield has a larger denominator than does their nominal yield; that means the current yield is lower.

85. **D)** Common stock is the most junior of the four securities mentioned, so it would fare the worst in bankruptcy. The mortgage bond would fare best in bankruptcy because it is secured with real collateral, and it pays a steady coupon, but it provides little or no exposure to equity upside. Cumulative preferred stock pays a dividend, but it can be irregular (although it accrues when

not paid). The convertible bond meets all the stated criteria; it pays a regular coupon and maintains exposure to equity upside because the bondholder can exchange the convertible bond for shares. Within the capital structure, the convertible bond is junior only to the mortgage bond. Option D is the clear choice based on the customer's preferences.

86. **C)** Money market securities are liquid, with minimal credit risk and short-term maturities. Commercial paper, or unsecured short-term promissory notes issued by corporations, represent one example of a money market security; Treasury bills represent another. Money market yields tend to be low, partly because they lack much credit risk and partly because they are short-term investments that reside at the front of the yield curve.

87. **C)** Corporate bond trades must be reported to the Trade Reporting and Compliance System (TRACE) as soon as practicable within 15 minutes of the consummation of the trade.

88. **B)** The Sharpe ratio is a metric that is commonly used in modern portfolio theory to characterize the ratio of return to risk (or variability) for a given strategy or portfolio. To compute the Sharpe ratio, standard deviation is frequently used as the descriptor of risk. The simplest approach is to divide mean return by standard deviation of returns. Thus, the strategy with the lower standard deviation—Strategy B—has a greater Sharpe ratio. All else being equal, a strategy with a greater Sharpe ratio is a more efficient way to profitably deploy capital.

89. **D)** The acid-test ratio is also known as the quick ratio because it divides short-term assets that the company can quickly liquidate by short-term liabilities that the company must pay within the next year. (The term *acid test* comes from the use of strong acids by miners to test whether a metal is gold.) A company with an acid-test ratio below 1 is not presently able to pay its short-term liabilities, and investors ought to approach it with caution. The acid-test ratio does not consider the value of inventory, which can be challenging to promptly liquidate.

90. **C)** This question involves three securities. The trader starts with QRS Oct 50-strike short puts, then owns QRS stock, then sells QRS Nov 50-strike calls. The QRS Oct 50-strike puts are sold at $1.30 each, or $390 total, and they are not bought back, so the options trader collects all of that premium. Three hundred shares of stock are bought for $50.00 per share and later sold at $50.00 per share, so there is neither a profit nor a loss from the stock itself. The QRS Nov 50-strike puts are sold at $2.00 each, or $600 total; they are not bought back, so the options trader (again) collects all of the premium. In other words, the 300 shares sell for the same price at which they were bought, and the trader collects the $990 total premium of all of the sold options. It is easy to get lost in the dollar figures of a problem that involves multiple prices. One approach to make this kind of problem easier is to think about each security rather than each transaction or each price.

91. **D)** Reinvestment risk is the potential that the holder of the security will receive cash flows (interest distributions, prepayment of principal, or dividend payments, for example) when those funds cannot be deployed at a similar yield. The callable bond can repay its face value at any time, depending on the preferences of the issuer, so the yield numbers are not important. The holder of a callable bond is at risk of interest rates falling, which would lead the issuer to call the bond. The issuer may do this using income from its business operations, or it may "refund" the callable bond by issuing new debt at a lower yield. If yields have declined, a bondholder whose bond gets called receives a lump sum of cash and no way to deploy it at the previous yield. In contrast, an issuer cannot forcibly call its common stock, nor can it call a bullet bond. A puttable bond can be repaid early at the election of the bondholder, but the issuer cannot compel the bondholder to do so. While coupon reinvestment is also a component of reinvestment risk, it is outweighed by the call risk of the bond described in Option D.

92. **C)** Like real estate investment trusts (REITs), Business Development Companies (BDCs) are a form of a regulated investment company that receives preferential tax treatment in exchange for meeting certain regulatory requirements and distributing the bulk of its investment income to its shareholders. Under the Investment Company Act of 1940, a BDC must satisfy a

variety of requirements, including investment of 70% or more of its holdings in "eligible" assets. For a public company to be considered an eligible portfolio company, the market capitalization of the public company's equity must be below $250 million.

93. **B)** Bond ratings can be divided into "investment grade" and "high yield," with the latter also described as "speculative," "noninvestment grade," or "junk." Of the three major rating agencies, S&P and Fitch use a rating scale that categorizes issues from AAA to D. Bonds categorized as BBB– or better are considered investment-grade securities. Bonds categorized as BB+ or worse are considered high-yield securities. (Moody's uses a slightly different scale, from AAA to C.)

94. **C)** Form U4 (Uniform Application for Securities Industry Registration or Transfer) is used to establish registration of an associated person. When a member firm must amend Form U4, it has a period of 30 days to do so. In cases where the amendment involves a statutory disqualification, that period is shortened to 10 days.

95. **D)** NYSE Group maintains cross-market circuit breakers that become active when the S&P 500 Index declines in value by a predetermined amount versus the prior trading day's closing value. For a Level 1 breach, the index must decline in value by 7%; for a Level 2 breach, 13%. If the index declines by 20%, a Level 3 breach is triggered, and the equities (and options) trading session will be halted for the remainder of the trading day across all NYSE Group exchanges. One way to remember these NYSE market-wide circuit breaker levels is to think of lucky 7, unlucky 13, and their sum of 20.

96. **A)** There are two components to this question: what the customer's interest is and which dealer provides a quotation for that interest. The customer is seeking an offer, so it can be concluded that the customer is interested in buying the security, eliminating Options C and D. Next, it must be determined which price is cheaper: the one quoted by Dealer A or by Dealer B. Assuming that the benchmark yield is 1.00%, Dealer A will sell at a yield of 1.20%, and Dealer B will sell at a yield of 1.18%. Yield and price have an inverse relationship: the higher the yield, the lower the price. From the perspective of a customer who is a buyer, the higher yield will cost less. Dealer A offers a better price because the yield spread is higher.

97. **C)** FINRA Rule 6460 establishes requirements for how and when a customer order must be displayed by an over-the-counter (OTC) market maker holding that order. Option C describes an odd-lot order and is thus exempt from the immediate display requirement. The order in Option A must be displayed because it substantially improves the size of the best bid in the inter-dealer quotation system. The order in Option B must be displayed because it improves on the offer price of the OTC market maker. The order in Option D improves on the price of the best offer in the inter-dealer quotation system, so it must be displayed.

98. **C)** Treasury bills are issued at a discount to par with maturities of 1 year or less and pay no coupons. Treasury notes have maturities of 2, 3, 5, 7, or 10 years. Treasury bonds have maturities of 20 or 30 years. Both Treasury notes and Treasury bonds pay coupons. Treasury Inflation-Protected Securities (TIPS) are issued with maturities of 5, 10, and 30 years, and TIPS pay coupons.

99. **A)** The Tax Reform Act of 1986 changed the tax treatment of municipal bonds held by banks, effectively removing preferential status for certain securities while establishing clear tax advantages for "bank-qualified" bonds. As a result, commercial banks' demand for nonqualified bonds diminished markedly. Issuances must meet certain requirements to be designated as bank-qualified: they generally must be smaller than $30 million and must serve a public purpose. Bank-qualified bonds tend to trade at a higher price than similar nonqualified bonds because they are limited in supply and their tax advantages compensate for a reduction in yield.

100. **B)** A clean price is the value of a bond without any accrued coupon interest; a dirty price is the clean price plus the accrued interest of the upcoming coupon. In the United States, corporate bonds are quoted at clean prices and transacted using dirty prices. Bond A recently

paid a coupon, and Bond B will imminently pay a coupon of 2/3 the nominal yield of Bond A but with a far greater accrual period. Compare 1 day of accrual at 3% nominal yield versus approximately 180 days of accrual at 2% nominal yield: the latter is greater. If Bonds A and B are trading at the same clean price, then the dirty price of Bond B will be richer because it carries more accrued interest.

101. **A)** By law, an investment company must make a written disclosure on a separate sheet of paper for dividends funded in whole or in part by sources other than net income for the previous year, net income for the current year, or accumulated undistributed net income.

102. **D)** With few exceptions, CBOE Rule 10.8 prohibits the practice of effecting a transaction that requires additional margin and attempting to furnish that margin "by liquidation of the same or other commitments." If the account requires additional margin, neither the transacted security nor other securities may be used to satisfy the requirement. That eliminates Options A and B. The solution suggested in Option C may reduce some risk exposure for the account, but in general it would increase the margin capital requirement. Option D appropriately resolves a margin call.

103. **C)** SEC Rule 35(d)-1, also known as the Names Rule, stipulates that investment companies may not have deceptive or misleading names. Investment companies whose names state a particular investment focus must maintain 80% or more of their assets invested in the stated area of focus.

104. **D)** By default, only expiring contracts that are in-the-money by a penny or more will be exercised. This process is called the "Exercise by Exception" (Ex-by-Ex) procedure by the Options Clearing Corp. (OCC). To override this default practice, a brokerage (or the member firm that clears its options transactions) may submit an instruction to either forcibly exercise or refrain from exercising an option. This instruction is formally known as a Contrary Exercise Advice. The OCC maintains an electronic system aptly named ENCORE for the purpose of swiftly communicating these last-minute instructions. The deadline for doing so is 5:30 p.m. EST on the last day of trading for the option.

105. **C)** A wash sale is the closure and reopening of a position (or a substantially similar position) within 30 days. Option D can be eliminated because it falls outside the scope of 30 days. Option A can be eliminated because long calls and long puts are not substantially similar; they express different views about the anticipated direction of stock price moves. Option B can be eliminated using the same logic, as long calls and short stock are not substantially similar positions. This leaves Option C, where long stock is sold and then a call option is purchased within 30 days.

106. **B)** A front-end load, also known as an initial sales charge, is deducted from an investment before the money is deployed. In contrast, a back-end load (or exit fee) is deducted from an investment upon closure of the position. Back-end loads charge a customer more for the investment if returns are positive than if returns are negative. Back-end loads that decrease gradually over time reward customers for leaving their money invested. To answer the question, first account for the 10% return of the investment that brings the total value of the customer's mutual fund position to $2,200,000. Three years pass before redemption, so the back-end load reduces (by 1% per year) to 2%, which amounts to $44,000. The total value of $2,200,000 minus this $44,000 back-end load is a net redemption of $2,156,000 for the customer.

107. **C)** Account information records must be preserved for at least 6 years from the date an account is closed. (Complaint records must be preserved for at least 3 years.)

108. **B)** SEC Rule 156 prohibits false or misleading content in an investment company's sales literature. This includes untrue statements, misleading statements, and omissions of material facts. Assertions that future returns can be inferred from past performance is one example of an untrue statement. Assurances that there is no downside risk is an example of a misleading statement. Failure to describe risks associated with the investment is an example of an omission of material fact.

109. **A)** The break-even price is the level in the underlying stock at which the intrinsic value of the option strategy is equal to the premium paid. In this case, the customer bought a QRS Jan 35 put and sold a QRS Jan 30 put. The option strategy cost $2.80. It would have an intrinsic value of $2.80 when the 35 put is in-the-money by that amount, which happens when QRS stock trades at $32.20 (35 − $2.80 = $32.20).

110. **C)** When a company authorizes a buyback, it purchases outstanding shares in the open market and commits them to its Treasury holdings. The amount of stock authorized for issuance should remain static at 1,000,000 shares. Treasury stock should increase from 100,000 shares to 300,000 shares. Outstanding stock should decrease from 500,000 shares to 300,000 shares.

111. **B)** The bond ratio equals the notional value of outstanding debt maturing in more than a year divided by that amount plus the equity capitalization of the company. The company has $200 million in outstanding debt maturing in more than a year, and its equity capitalization is $600 million, so its bond ratio is ($200,000,000 ÷ $800,000,000), or 1/4.

112. **D)** Build America Bonds were established by the American Recovery and Reinvestment Act of 2009 in response to concerns about reduced confidence in the ability of state and local governments to access capital in debt markets. These bonds came in two versions, one involving direct payments from the federal government to issuers in the amount of 35% of the issuer's interest costs, and another granting tax credits to bondholders for 35% of interest costs. These bonds could not be issued by private institutions, and they could only be used for the same purposes permitted for tax-exempt municipal bonds. By making Build America Bonds federally taxable (unlike other municipal bonds), the federal government gave a broader group of market participants an incentive to buy Build America Bonds.

113. **A)** Regulation S exempts debt issuances that are offered to and bought by non-US-located buyers from registration with the SEC. Rule 144a does not apply when a security is offered to individual investors; a 144a security can be purchased only by Qualified Institutional Buyers (QIBs). Rule 504 of Regulation D is intended for small issuances; it does not apply to issuances that exceed $5 million in a 12-month period. Section 3(a)(2) applies to bank note programs.

114. **A)** Dividends are not paid to treasury stock; they are also not paid to unissued shares. The full dividend distribution of $11 million will be distributed across CDE's ten million outstanding shares, amounting to a per-share dividend of $1.10 ($11,000,000 ÷ 10,000,000 = $1.10).

115. **B)** Special purpose acquisition companies (SPACs), also known as blank-check companies, are publicly listed companies with no stated business operations. They exist only to merge with or acquire another company. A unit investment trust (UIT) maintains a particular, usually fixed, portfolio of securities designed around a stated investment objective in a buy-and-hold strategy; investors can purchase units of the total portfolio. A direct participation program is a pooled investment whereby limited partners can invest in businesses without taking on the personal liability assumed by the general partners who manage the business operations of the entity. The Depository Trust & Clearing Corporation is the most active clearinghouse and settlement processor for financial markets in the United States.

116. **C)** The maximum potential loss of a vertical put (or call) credit spread is the difference between the strikes minus the premium collected. To establish a VWX Dec 22/11 put credit spread, an investor sells a VWX Dec 22 put and buys a VWX Dec 11 put. The maximum intrinsic value of a 22/11 put spread is $11.00, but the trader collected a $5.44 credit on the way into the trade. $11.00 − $5.44 = $5.56; using the 100 multiplier, it is $556.

117. **C)** Noninstitutional customer transactions for corporate or agency debt securities must be accompanied by confirmations that include the exact time of the transaction, so Option C is correct. According to FINRA Rule 2232, markup (or markdown) disclosure is NOT required as part of the transaction confirmation when a broker-dealer acquires securities as part of a fixed-price offering and sells them at the public offering price (POP) on the same day. Finally,

a corporate bond is generally not considered a national market system (NMS) security by the SEC. Usually, there is no way to observe a National Best Bid and Offer (NBBO) for these securities.

118. **C)** A NYSE 72(d) crossing transaction allows a floor broker to match customer orders without giving priority to existing bids or offers at the same price. For a NYSE 72(d) cross to take place, the transaction must meet either a minimum size of 10,000 shares (ruling out Options B and D) or a minimum market value of $200,000. The fact that the customer's order is "not held" means that the floor broker can exercise time and price discretion to sell 25,000 shares, and execute smaller pieces as he sees fit, at or above the limit price. However, the floor broker cannot execute worse than the customer's limit price, so the order in Option A cannot trade against the customer's offer under any circumstances. The bid in Option C, on the other hand, meets the size requirement while also bidding higher than the customer's limit offer of $19.90.

119. **C)** According to FINRA Rule 12206, claims submitted for arbitration cannot postdate the alleged violation by more than 6 years. However, this limitation does not preclude legal action in court for grievances that took place more than 6 years prior. In fact, a party that succeeds in having a FINRA arbitration claim dismissed using Rule 12206 agrees that the claimant has a right to pursue the grievance (and any related grievances) in court.

120. **D)** SPX options expire versus the morning settlement level of the S&P 500 Index, which consists of 500 stocks, in a variety of sectors, weighted by market capitalization. SPX options settle as cash. This contrasts with single-stock options (and ETF options) that settle as physical shares. For example, a holder of SPX in-the-money calls has no residual risk when the calls are exercised because her options turn into cash on the morning of the expiration date. However, holders of SPY in-the-money calls remain exposed to directional moves in the underlying SPY ETF after exercise because their options turn into shares of SPY on the afternoon of the expiration date. This distinction is vital to keep in mind when making decisions about how best to hedge risk.

121. **A)** Suitable large investments for a customer who is hoping to retire soon typically involve low-risk exposure and seek to appreciate modestly rather than generate outsized returns. Wildcatting is the practice of exploring for new oil reserves by drilling in places that have not been demonstrated to harbor petroleum—a high-reward but high-risk endeavor. Unlike more diversified petroleum companies, a direct participation program (DPP) established for the sole purpose of prospecting for oil may not be a suitable large investment for a person who intends to retire soon and who lacks the ability to absorb losses without making lifestyle changes. The core assets of a Treasury bill exchange-traded fund (ETF) have little to no risk of default. A high-dividend-yield ETF is also low risk: companies with large dividend distributions are often mature, and packaging them together in one product provides diversification. A tower real estate investment trust (REIT) passes income from radio tower leases to shareholders, which may have some geographic diversification but lacks diversification across business segments; still, it is a far safer investment than a wildcatting DPP.

122. **A)** Treasury bills are federal government bond issues that mature within a year or less of issuance. They do not pay coupons and are instead issued at a discount to par.

123. **B)** BrokerCheck is a tool for transparency and a central repository of information about employment history, registration exam history, and disciplinary actions. However, information reported only in Section 3 ("Reason for Termination") of Form U5 is not disclosed through BrokerCheck when an associated person leaves employment with a member.

124. **C)** The product being pitched is an agency collateralized mortgage obligation (CMO). FINRA Rule 2216 controls the content and presentation of retail communications regarding CMO products. Options A, B, and D describe requirements imposed as part of Rule 2216; however, retail communications regarding CMOs are not permitted to compare the CMO to any other investment product, not even to a bank certificate of deposit (CD).

125. **D)** Naked calls are dangerous because their potential losses have no strict bounds. If the stock rallies, a short squeeze takes place or another company can acquire XYZ at a very rich premium; a naked call can generate steep and painful losses that exceed both the current price of the stock and the trader's posted margin. This potential for loss is infinite because a stock price can always increase further if demand for the stock exceeds the supply at the current price.

126. **B)** For a person or group to exercise discretionary power in a customer account, FINRA requires members to receive the customer's written authorization, and also requires members to record the signature(s) of the empowered person or group. This information must be recorded along with the date that discretionary power is granted. A termination date of discretionary power is not required to be set.

127. **D)** In a rights offering, shareholders have a brief period of time to decide whether they want to exercise the right to buy more shares for a set price, called the subscription price. The subscription price is typically lower than the market price of the stock. A few shareholders may even consider the consequences if a company is unable to raise funds in the equity market. These consequences may include a subsequent rights offering at a lower price in the equity market or a bond issuance in the debt market. Any combination of these reasons could potentially motivate a shareholder to buy shares directly from the company in a rights offering rather than in the secondary market.

128. **A)** A bond counsel is a lawyer or legal firm that generates key documents, secures required approvals, and performs all other legal functions required for a municipal bond issue to take place. The selection of a bond counsel begins with a request for proposal (RFP) distributed by the issuer. This is true even when the issuer is raising capital for a third party ("conduit borrower") to use for a public benefit.

129. **C)** Absent interest rate effects and dividends, with the stock trading in the same place as it was when the straddle traded for $8.42, and an unchanged implied volatility for the option, the straddle has only one changed input: time. As time passes, a straddle loses value because options are worth more when they grant the option holder more time to make a decision. Because the straddle is made up of 1 long call and 1 long put, it will lose value after a month passes because of theta (time decay).

130. **C)** One key difference between a bullet bond and an asset-backed security (ABS) is that there is no prepayment risk on the former, while the latter carries an assumption of prepayment rates. If the prepayment rate of the assets in an ABS exceeds this assumption, then the total return of the security will be less than expected because the average life of the stream of principal cash flows will be shorter. ABS investors charge a premium to compensate for the risk that they will get their money back earlier than expected, and thus lose the chance to collect future interest payments.

131. **B)** Option chains typically show a continuous and two-sided quotation for each contract. These displayed quotations can be combined to determine the best bid and offer for an option strategy. The question asks for the offer price of a bull call spread, a strategy that consists of a long GHIJ Dec 40 call and a short GHIJ Dec 45 call. The GHIJ Dec 40 call is offered at a debit of $1.50, and the bid for the GHIJ Dec 45 call is a credit of $0.10. An investor who buys the GHIJ Dec 40/45 bull call spread at the displayed offer will pay a net debit of $1.40 for the strategy (not including commissions) because $1.50 – $0.10 = $1.40.

132. **A)** FINRA establishes disclosure requirements for investment analysis tools. One such requirement is a description of the methodology and criteria used, including the limitations and assumptions thereof. Software is permitted to exclude or favor certain investments, as long as the reasons are explained in writing. Analysis results may depend on constantly changing factors like market contexts, user-generated inputs, and randomized characteristics, and the fact that results may vary with each use and over time must be disclosed in writing. Software is not expected to predict the future, and the hypothetical nature of its predictive analysis must be clearly disclosed using specific language.

133. **D)** With few exceptions—all of which must be unavoidable, documented, and explained—FINRA rules disallow an associated person who performs a supervisory role from supervising their own activities. Furthermore, no associated person may supervise people who make decisions about their compensation and continued employment.

134. **C)** Special cash dividends are not distributed on a regular schedule. Option strikes are typically adjusted for special cash dividends that exceed $12.50 per option contract (in other words, 12.5 cents per share of stock). Options traders thus need not speculate about the amount or timing of a special dividend; they are also protected from losses due to uneconomical early exercise decisions based on incomplete information. The Options Clearing Corp. (OCC) determines the criteria and characteristics for these adjustments. Typically, the strike of an option contract is adjusted downward on the ex-dividend date by the amount of a large special cash dividend.

135. **D)** The bond, which is an original issue discount (OID) bond, must be accreted (interest earned would be the difference between par—$1,000—and the OID, which was $960). Holding the bond to maturity would result in $40 earned over the 20-year period ($2 per year). The bond was held for 8 years, so the total accretion is $16 (8 years × $2 per year). This accretion is added to the original cost. The difference between the sale price ($920) and the cost as adjusted ($976) indicates a $56 loss to the seller.

3 Practice Test 3

1. What disclosure document is provided with a Regulation D offering?
   A) offering memorandum
   B) prospectus
   C) private placement memorandum
   D) official statement

2. An underwriting in which the stock issue is canceled if it is not completely sold is called what?
   A) standby
   B) best efforts
   C) all-or-none
   D) internal commitment

3. Which type of order may be accepted by a specialist?
   A) not held
   B) good-till-canceled
   C) good-through-week
   D) good-through-month

4. A dealer in an eastern syndicate has a 10% participation in a municipal underwriting of $3 million. The dealer sells its entire allotment, but $1 million remains unsold. The dealer is liable for what amount of the unsold bonds?
   A) $0
   B) $100,000
   C) $200,000
   D) $300,000

5. In the NYSE Bond quote yield column, what does the notation cv mean?
   A) convertible bond
   B) deep discount
   C) yield not available
   D) zero coupon

6. What percentage of the purchase price must a buyer of an option pay?
   A) 25%
   B) 30%
   C) 50%
   D) 100%

7. In May, a customer buys 100 XYZ common stock at $70 per share and buys 1 XYZ Aug 70 put for $4. At expiration, the customer sells his shares of XYZ at $80 per share, and the put expires worthless. What is the customer's profit or loss?
   A) $400
   B) $600
   C) $1,000
   D) $1,400

8. What is the first source of funding for public housing revenue bonds?
   A) income derived from rents
   B) government backing
   C) proceeds from future issues
   D) ad valorem taxes

9. A customer with no existing securities positions buys an option. Later in the week, she chooses to liquidate the position by writing an option with the same contract terms as the option previously bought. What is this transaction called?

    A) opening sale
    B) closing sale
    C) open interest
    D) closing purchase

10. If a customer buys 100 shares of XYZ common stock when the current market value is $80 per share and later buys a put, which of the following would be correct?

    A) The customer has created a married put.
    B) The customer has established a covered put.
    C) The customer is hedging against a price decline.
    D) The customer may have an unlimited loss.

11. An investor purchases 1 XYZ Jun 55 call for $4 when the stock is at $53. If the stock rises to $60 and he exercises the call, the investor will

    A) own the stock at a cost basis of $51 per share.
    B) enjoy a $200 profit.
    C) face a $400 loss.
    D) own the stock at a cost basis of $59 per share.

12. A customer wants to sell 10 uncovered XYZ Jun 40 calls at $4\frac{3}{4}$ when the underlying stock is trading at $42. If she covers the options at $2\frac{1}{8}$, what is the gain?

    A) $2,225
    B) $2,625
    C) $4,000
    D) $4,750

13. Retained earnings represent what on a corporate balance sheet?

    A) shareholder's equity
    B) capital surplus
    C) undistributed net income
    D) working capital

14. According to Options Clearing Corp. rules, each investor or group of investors is limited in the number of listed option contracts that may be held on the same side of the market with the same underlying stock. What is the maximum number that may be held without a special written authorization?

    A) 2,000
    B) 5,000
    C) 25,000
    D) 250,000

15. Which of the following is an advantage in an oil and gas drilling limited partnership?

    A) severable liability for general partners
    B) depletion allowance
    C) all investors have a say in day-to-day management
    D) limited risk of capital for general partners

16. A customer wants to sell 10 uncovered XYZ Jun 40 calls at $4\frac{3}{4}$ when the underlying stock is trading at $42.00. What is her breakeven?

    A) $35.25
    B) $40.00
    C) $44.75
    D) $46.75

17. A company is being sued for $10 billion. If the company prevails, the stock price will probably increase. If the company is unsuccessful, it may go out of business. The company's stock would be considered what?

    A) blue chip
    B) growth
    C) defensive
    D) special situation

18. A customer purchases 1 MNO 70 call for $4 and 1 MNO 70 put for $2, with MNO trading at $72. If MNO moves to $81 upon expiration, what is the profit or loss (assuming exercise of the call)?

    A) $500 profit
    B) $500 loss
    C) $600 profit
    D) $600 loss

19. A customer purchases 1 XYZ 40 call for $6 and sells 1 XYZ 50 call at $3. The price of XYZ stock is trading at $39. What is the break-even point for this position?
    A) $34
    B) $38
    C) $43
    D) $47

20. A customer purchases a municipal bond at $97 in secondary trading, with the bond maturing in 10 years. She sells the bond after 5 years for $103. What is her gain or loss on sale?
    A) no gain or loss
    B) $30 gain
    C) $45 gain
    D) $60 gain

21. A customer sells 1 ABC 30 call at $3 and 1 ABC 30 put at $5 with the price of ABC trading at $27. What is the maximum gain for this position?
    A) $300
    B) $400
    C) $600
    D) $800

22. A customer has $10,000 to invest and wants to buy a government security at a discount, with a maturity in 3 months. Which government security should the investor purchase?
    A) Treasury bills
    B) Treasury notes
    C) Treasury bonds
    D) Treasury receipts

23. A mature company that is in a stable industry and whose stock provides investors with a relatively high dividend yield has what type of stock?
    A) growth
    B) cyclical
    C) income
    D) speculative

24. A put writer sold a 35 XYZ put for $2.25 with no position in the underlying stock. What is the maximum loss for this option position?
    A) $225
    B) $3,275
    C) $3,500
    D) unlimited

25. A security is registered in the names of A. Jones and Mrs. B. Jones. The certificates can be endorsed by
    A) A. Jones only.
    B) either A. Jones or Mrs. B. Jones.
    C) Mrs. B. Jones only.
    D) A. Jones and Mrs. B. Jones jointly.

26. An individual investor looking to receive a pro rata share of company dividends and the ability to vote for members of the board of directors should purchase what type of stock?
    A) common stock
    B) preferred stock
    C) prior preferred stock
    D) convertible preferred stock

27. Given the end-of-day price Thursday, August 15, an investor who purchased 300 shares of Investors Fund on the morning of Thursday, August 15, would have paid a total of what?

Fund Name	NAV	POP	Net Asset Change
Investors Fund	$5.60	$6.03	+0.02
Wealth Fund	$7.80	$8.50	+0.01

    A) $1,680
    B) $1,680 plus sales charge
    C) $1,809
    D) $1,809 plus sales charge

28. An investor purchasing a bond with no pledge of specific collateral that is backed by the full faith and credit of the issuer has purchased what type of bond?
    A) equipment trust certificate
    B) mortgage bond
    C) debenture
    D) income bond

29. GNMA securities are guaranteed by the full faith and credit of the US government, which ensures what?
    A) payment of the principal only
    B) payment of the principal, interest, and late payment
    C) timely payment of principal only
    D) timely payment of principal and interest

30. If a customer has an inactive account with a cash balance and no securities, how frequently must statements of account be sent?
    A) monthly
    B) quarterly
    C) semiannually
    D) annually

31. If the opening transaction in a customer's account is the purchase of $10,000 ABC convertible bonds at par, under Regulation T, how much cash must be deposited?
    A) $2,000
    B) $2,500
    C) $5,000
    D) $10,000

32. In the OTC market, what is the difference between a market maker's bid and ask prices called?
    A) spread
    B) markup
    C) markdown
    D) commission

33. A 10% par convertible bond is issued convertible at $50.00 a share when the parity price of the bond is $975. What is the parity price of the stock?
    A) $19.50
    B) $48.75
    C) $49.36
    D) $50.00

34. The funds accumulated in a sinking fund may be used for all of the following EXCEPT
    A) to redeem the bonds at maturity.
    B) to exercise a partial call.
    C) to pay a dividend to bondholders.
    D) to repurchase bonds in open market.

35. What does a greenshoe allow an underwriter to do?
    A) oversubscribe an offering by up to 15%
    B) undersubscribe an offering despite a firm commitment
    C) lend shares to short-selling customers before an IPO
    D) receive a limited number of preferred shares in exchange for fully subscribing an offering

36. What is the redemption price of an open-end investment company?
    A) NAV + SC
    B) NAV
    C) POP
    D) determined by the market

37. To what does the Trust Indenture Act of 1939 apply?
    A) corporate bond offerings in a single state
    B) multistate corporate bond offering
    C) US government securities
    D) multistate common stock offering

38. What is the difference between an open-end investment company and a closed-end investment company?
    A) investment objective
    B) fund management
    C) fund capitalization
    D) method used to calculate the NAV

39. What is the most important suitability consideration for a client who chooses to purchase a variable annuity?
    A) Monthly payments will remain fixed.
    B) There will be a penalty for the early withdrawal of funds.
    C) Assumed interest rate (AIR) will vary.
    D) Benefit payments will vary.

40. What risk is associated with a security that may lose value due to a drop in stock prices?
    A) credit risk
    B) market risk
    C) capital risk
    D) call risk

41. Who is responsible for ensuring that dividends and proxy information are distributed to the correct party after a shareholder sells his shares to another investor?
    A) officers of the issuing corporation
    B) brokerages of the buyer and seller
    C) the exchange where the shares traded
    D) the transfer agent and registrar

42. Which of the following circumstances would allow the management of a mutual fund to change the investment objectives of the fund?
    A) The shareholders have been given 30 days' prior notification.
    B) The shareholders have been given the right to switch funds at no expense with objectives similar to those the fund presently has.
    C) The fund's NAV has declined by more than 50% of the original offering price.
    D) Fifty percent of the fund's shareholders holding the outstanding voting securities have given authorization.

43. Which of the following is NOT a characteristic of preferred stock?
    A) company ownership
    B) a fixed and guaranteed rate of return
    C) perpetuity
    D) priority over common stock for dividends

44. A 12b-1 fee is which of the following?
    A) a fee on a buy or sell transaction, charged by the broker to the investor
    B) an annual marketing or distribution fee on a mutual fund
    C) an annual fee assessed to a mutual fund's director, unless the director has less than $1 million in investable assets
    D) any fee on a mutual fund that is over 1% of the fund's net assets

45. Which of the following statements is CORRECT regarding the relationship between the yields of the Bond Buyer 20 Bond Index and the Bond Buyer 11 Bond Index?
    A) The yield on the 11 Bond Index is lower than the yield on the 20 Bond Index.
    B) The yield on the 11 Bond Index is the same as the yield on the 20 Bond Index.
    C) The yield on the 11 Bond Index is higher than the yield on the 20 Bond Index.
    D) There is no relationship between the yields of the 11 Bond Index and the 20 Bond Index.

46. Which of the following terms are paired when liquidating open-end investment company shares that have a sales charge?
    A) ask price; sales price
    B) sales price; NAV
    C) NAV; sales redemption price
    D) bid price; public offering price

47. Which of the following would take place if a customer enters an order to purchase 300 shares of ACME stock at $20 per share, is informed that the shares were purchased at $19, and later discovers that the trade was executed at $20?
    A) The registered representative would be required to make up the difference using an error account.
    B) The floor broker would be required to make up the difference if the mistake was made by the floor broker.
    C) The trade would be busted and reprinted at $19.
    D) The customer would be required to pay the execution price of $20 per share for ACME stock.

48. Which system is used by broker-dealers trading over-the-counter equities that are NOT listed on the NASDAQ?
    A) green sheets
    B) blue sheets
    C) pink sheets
    D) yellow sheets

49. A company has convertible bonds outstanding with a conversion price of $25.00. If there is an anti-dilution clause in the trust indenture, what would be the effect of a 10% stock dividend?
    A) Bondholders would receive a check for $50.00.
    B) Bondholders would receive 4 shares of the common stock.
    C) The conversion price would be reduced to $22.72.
    D) There would be no effect.

50. A customer with no other securities positions sells 1 ABC Sep 30 put to collect a premium of $3. At the time of the trade, the price of ABC stock is $30 per share. If the position is assigned when the stock falls to $25 per share, what is the mark-to-market profit or loss?
    A) $100 profit
    B) $100 loss
    C) $200 profit
    D) $200 loss

51. A customer's first transaction in a margin account is a purchase of 100 shares of ABC for $50 per share. Under Regulation T, what is the customer's initial equity requirement?
    A) $1,000
    B) $1,500
    C) $2,500
    D) $5,000

52. A customer purchases 1 JKL 75 put for $4 and sells 1 JKL 85 put at $8 in a cash account with the price of JKL trading at $79. What is the maximum gain for this position?
    A) $200
    B) $400
    C) $600
    D) $800

53. What does UGMA stand for?
    A) Uniform Grant to Minors Act
    B) Uniform Grant to Minorities Act
    C) Uniform Gifts to Minors Act
    D) Uniform Gifts to Minorities Act

54. A customer receiving interest income from holding a qualified private activity bond would MOST likely pay which of the following taxes?
    A) ordinary income tax
    B) alternative minimum tax
    C) capital gains tax
    D) excise taxes

55. In April, a customer sells 1 ABC Jul 40 call at $5 and buys 1 ABC Nov 40 call for $8. Closing transactions are executed in late June with the purchase of 1 ABC Jul 40 call for $2 and sale of 1 ABC Nov 40 call at $6. What is the profit or loss?
    A) $100 profit
    B) $100 loss
    C) $300 profit
    D) $300 loss

56. A stock's tangible NAV per share is the same as its
    A) book value.
    B) market value.
    C) par value.
    D) stated value.

57. Which of the following is an advantage of CMOs over GNMA securities?
    A) a longer-than-expected average life
    B) favorable tax treatment
    C) no correlation risk
    D) a steadier cash flow

58. How are customer securities valued in a liquidation under SIPC?
    A) by their current market value at the date of distribution
    B) by the customers' original cost basis
    C) by their current market value at the time of liquidation
    D) by the lower of the customers' cost basis or fair market value

59. A customer purchases both an Apr 20 ABC put and an Apr 20 ABC call. This method is known as what?
    A) short straddle
    B) long straddle
    C) vertical spread
    D) long strangle

60. What amount of capital may be raised through a Rule 505 offering?
    A) $500,000
    B) $1,000,000
    C) $1,500,000
    D) $5,000,000

61. What is the largest monthly payment to the holder of a variable annuity that will occur under the following payout options?
    A) life annuity payment
    B) life annuity period certain payment
    C) joint life annuity payment
    D) unit refund life annuity payment

62. What risk is associated with investment-grade bonds?
    A) credit risk
    B) selection risk
    C) inflationary risk
    D) timing risk

63. What would be used when analyzing the sources of revenue and expenses in a limited partnership?
    A) analysis of capital
    B) analysis of cash flow
    C) analysis of liquidity
    D) analysis of the portfolio

64. Which of the following BEST describes a restricted long account?
    A) above 50% initial margin requirements; below 25% maintenance level
    B) above 50% initial margin requirements; below 30% maintenance level
    C) below 50% initial margin; above the 25% maintenance level
    D) below 50% initial margin requirements; above the 30% maintenance level

65. A customer opens an account and makes a purchase of 300 shares of XYZ for $60. Subsequently, XYZ increases to $64 per share, then decreases to $58 per share. Assuming the starting balance equals the Regulation T initial margin requirement, the equity and SMA in the account will be which of the following?
    A) $8,400 equity; $0 SMA
    B) $8,400 equity; $600 SMA
    C) $9,000; $0 SMA
    D) $10,200 equity; $600 SMA

66. Which of the following investments would BEST be used as a hedge against inflation?
    A) corporate bonds
    B) series EE bonds
    C) variable annuities
    D) face-amount certificates

67. Which of the following statements is CORRECT concerning American-style stock options?
    A) An American stock option must be exercised before expiration.
    B) The seller of a put may be compelled to purchase 100 shares of the underlying security.
    C) At expiration, a stock option will become a market order for the underlying security.
    D) The buyer of a put has a bearish outlook of the market.

68. A company is calling the preferred stock it issued for $102. The preferred stock is convertible into four shares of common stock, which is trading at $20 per share. What should the holder of the preferred stock do?
    A) allow the preferred stock to be called by the company
    B) do nothing because the company cannot force shareholders to sell the preferred stock
    C) convert the preferred stock into shares of common stock
    D) sell the preferred stock to someone else at $100

69. A customer with no other securities positions sells 1 ABC Sep 30 put at a premium of $3 when the price of ABC stock is $30 per share. What would the stock price of ABC need to be just before expiration for the customer to break even?

   A) $30
   B) $27
   C) $25
   D) $20

70. In how many days do municipal bonds settle regular way?

   A) 1 day
   B) 2 days
   C) 3 days
   D) 5 days

71. The sales load of a mutual fund is 8.0% and has a 1.5% underwriter's concession. If the NAV is $16.50, the offering price is determined by dividing the NAV by what?

   A) 91.5%
   B) 92.0%
   C) 108.0%
   D) 115.0%

72. A customer purchases 1 MNO 70 call for $4 and 1 MNO 70 put for $2, with MNO trading at $72. What is the maximum loss?

   A) $0
   B) $300
   C) $500
   D) $600

73. A customer sells 1 ABC 30 call at $3 and 1 ABC 30 put at $5, with the price of ABC trading at $28. If the price of ABC moves to $19 upon expiration and the customer receives an exercise notice for the put, what is the total profit or loss?

   A) $800 profit
   B) $300 profit
   C) $800 loss
   D) $300 loss

74. A customer sells 1 ABC Jul 40 call at $5 and buys 1 ABC Nov 40 call for $8. What is the break-even price for this calendar call spread, assuming the Jul call expires worthless?

   A) $37
   B) $40
   C) $43
   D) $48

75. What cost basis applies to the recipient when an investor gives a gift of his shares in ABC Corporation to his brother's adult son?

   A) fair market value on date of transfer
   B) zero
   C) giver's original cost basis
   D) no tax is paid on securities received as a gift

76. A registered representative sells a stake in a master limited partnership. However, her firm is not offering or overseeing the sale of that security, nor has the firm granted her written permission for the sale. What is this practice known as?

   A) disintermediation
   B) selling away
   C) hypothecation
   D) front-running

77. When does an equity trade between two brokers or dealers settle?

   A) trade date (T + 0)
   B) business day after the trade date (T + 1)
   C) 2 business days after trade date (T + 2)
   D) 7 business days after trade date (T + 7)

78. In February 2014, an investor bought 100 shares of Company ABC, which pays no dividends, at $50 a share. In April 2015, he decides to sell 100 shares of Company ABC at $40 a share. How will his trade be taxed and on what amount?

   A) on a short-term capital gain of $10 per share
   B) on a long-term capital loss of $500 per share
   C) on a long-term capital loss of $10 per share
   D) on a short-term capital gain of $500 per share

79. General Corp. has a 10% bond outstanding. A customer owns one bond purchased for $1,100. When the next interest payment date occurs, what will the customer receive?

    A) $50
    B) $55
    C) $100
    D) $110

80. Volatility for the share price of an acquisition target tends to decrease the most in which of the following transaction structures?

    A) all cash
    B) all stock
    C) cash and stock
    D) none of the above

81. Prior preferred stock provides what benefits?

    A) It is issued before the regular preferred.
    B) Asset liquidation has priority over bonds.
    C) Share convertibility to debt is at par value.
    D) Dividends have priority over common and preferred stock.

82. A customer purchases 1 JKL 75 put for $4 and sells 1 JKL 85 put at $8 in a cash account with the price of JKL trading at $79. What is the maximum loss?

    A) $200
    B) $400
    C) $600
    D) $800

83. Which of the following groups establishes blue sky laws to protect investors from fraud?

    A) Congress
    B) states
    C) municipalities
    D) FINRA

84. What are the Regulation T and FINRA initial margin and minimum maintenance margin requirements for long stock in margin accounts?

    A) 25% / 30%
    B) 50% / 25%
    C) 50% / 30%
    D) 50% / 50%

85. An investment company with no management fee and a relatively low percentage sales charge invested in a fixed portfolio of municipal or corporate bonds is called what?

    A) closed-end investment company
    B) open-end investment company
    C) unit investment trust
    D) face-amount certificate company

86. Which of the following is often the largest operating expense in a money market fund, typically ranging from 0.2% to over 2.0% of assets under management?

    A) custodial fee
    B) fee for auditing services
    C) registration fees and taxes
    D) management fees and advisory fees

87. What is the purpose of an illustration of rates of return in variable life insurance sales literature?

    A) to give customers a prediction of investment profits or losses under various market conditions
    B) to give customers a comparison of variable life insurance to other investment alternatives
    C) to show customers how performance in the investment account may affect death benefits and cash values
    D) to show customers what payments they should expect

88. A broker who extends credit for the purpose of purchasing or carrying margin stocks must comply with what rules?

    A) Regulation G
    B) Regulation T
    C) Regulation D
    D) Regulation X

89. When an investor purchases a municipal bond at a premium, the book value of the bond is decreased during the bond's holding period. What is this accounting process known as?

    A) depreciation of capital
    B) amortization of capital
    C) accretion of discount
    D) accrual of interest

90. Which of the following bonds will have the greatest change in price when interest rates increase from 8% to 10%?

    A) an 8% bond maturing in 2 years
    B) an 8% bond maturing in 5 years
    C) an 8% bond maturing in 7 years
    D) an 8% bond maturing in 10 years

91. A customer purchases a 25 call for a premium of $3. What is the breakeven for this option?

    A) $22
    B) $25
    C) $28
    D) $32

92. Which of the following is true for individuals, regardless of their income level, who are active participants in an employer-sponsored qualified retirement plan?

    A) Contributions are allowed for Roth IRAs but not for traditional IRAs.
    B) Contributions to a Roth or traditional IRA are allowed.
    C) Contributions to an IRA are allowed but can never be deducted from gross income.
    D) Contributions to an IRA are allowed and can always be deducted from gross income.

93. Fixed-maturity securities are typically BEST described as which of the following?

    A) They provide fixed, periodic payments.
    B) They do not return the principal upon maturity.
    C) They are typically stocks or preferred stocks.
    D) They have payments that vary according to prime rate fluctuations.

94. A customer purchased an 8% bond with a yield to maturity of 9%, then sold it several years later. The yield to maturity on the bond is 7%. The customer has

    A) a 2% loss.
    B) a loss on the sale.
    C) a gain on the sale.
    D) no gain or loss.

95. A company is involved in a rights offering with a subscription price of $43.00 per share, where the company's current stock market price is $45.00 per share. Three rights purchase one share of the company's common stock. The rights are currently trading at $0.75 per right. If the customer does not want to own the company's stock, but she does want to purchase some rights for speculative reasons, she should be advised that

    A) the profit opportunity is immediate.
    B) market value of the shares must increase more for the investment to be profitable.
    C) there is no profit opportunity available.
    D) a rights offering is not an appropriate strategy for speculation.

96. A customer gave a registered representative $15,000 with instructions to "buy whatever tech stock you think is best and let me know when you're done." The registered representative must

    A) follow the customer's verbal instructions.
    B) ask the customer to repeat the verbal authorization to the representative's branch manager.
    C) accept the customer's verbal instructions only if the registered representative is registered as an investment adviser.
    D) obtain a signed and firm-approved discretionary disclosure from the customer before executing the instructions.

97. A customer sells 1 ABC 30 call at $3 and 1 ABC 30 put at $5, with the price of ABC trading at $28. If the price of ABC moves to $45 upon the expiration date and the customer receives an exercise notice for the 30 call, what is his profit or loss?

    A) $700 loss
    B) $700 profit
    C) $800 loss
    D) $800 profit

98. If a home has an assessed valuation of $1 million, with a tax rate of 5 mills, what is the homeowner's tax liability?

    A) $5
    B) $50
    C) $500
    D) $5,000

99. An investor bought a long-term equity anticipation security (LEAPS) call contract for $6.40. Now, 16 months later, she sells the call at $9.00. For the relevant taxable year, her long-term capital gains tax is 20%, and her short-term capital gains tax is 37%. How much tax does she owe on the proceeds from this LEAPS call?

   A) $52.00
   B) $96.20
   C) $180.00
   D) $333.00

100. One contract of a put with a strike price of $30 is purchased for a premium of $3. What is its maximum profit?

   A) $27
   B) $30
   C) $2,700
   D) $3,000

101. A market maker is asked by a customer for a firm offer on 1,000 shares of XYZ Corp stock. The market maker provides a quote of $15.46. The customer promptly responds by placing a limit order to buy 1,000 shares of XYZ Corp stock for $15.46 or better, but the market maker does not fill the order before the closing bell. Which term BEST describes the action of the firm holding XYZ Corp stock?

   A) interpositioning
   B) hypothecation
   C) disintermediation
   D) backing away

102. An increase in the price of open-end investment shares from the initial purchase is called what?

   A) accretion
   B) amortization
   C) appreciation
   D) capital gain

103. An investor owns a US government security with a 20-year maturity and interest coupons attached. What type of security does the investor own?

   A) Treasury bills
   B) Treasury notes
   C) Treasury bonds
   D) Treasury receipts

104. General Manufacturing Corp. has a $6 preferred stock that is outstanding. Which of the following statements is true?

   A) Par value is $100 per share.
   B) There is no par value.
   C) The issue is considered prior preferred.
   D) The issue can be converted into common stock at $6 per share.

105. In a customer's account, the opening transaction is the purchase of $10,000 ABC convertible bonds at par. If the bonds appreciated to 110, what would the SMA be?

   A) $50
   B) $100
   C) $500
   D) $1,000

106. To create a limited partnership, which of the following must be filed with the state?

   A) limited partnership agreement
   B) limited partnership certificate
   C) subscription agreement
   D) underwriting agreement

107. The fees that a firm charges for services must adhere to what standard?

   A) They must be first approved by FINRA.
   B) They must represent a fair and reasonable charge.
   C) They may not exceed 5%.
   D) They must be based on what the market can bear.

108. The Instinet system relates to what?

   A) first market trading
   B) second market trading
   C) third market trading
   D) fourth market trading

109. Which tranche of a sequential pay CMO with three tranches (A, B, and C) has the highest contraction risk?

   A) tranche A
   B) tranche B
   C) tranche C
   D) tranche Z

110. A tax-exempt security is typically characterized by which of the following?
    A) always exempt from city, state, and federal tax
    B) exempt from city, state, and federal tax, depending on the date of purchase
    C) usually exempt from city, state, and federal tax, depending on where the investor lives
    D) usually exempt from city, state, and federal tax, depending on the investor's tax bracket

111. What is the minimum equity requirement for a pattern day trader with no other securities positions who bought $10,000 of a security and sold all of it later on the same day?
    A) $5,000
    B) $10,000
    C) $25,000
    D) $100,000

112. What type of variable annuity payout option would allow a couple to continue receiving income for the second individual upon the death of the first?
    A) life annuity payments
    B) life annuity period certain payments
    C) life annuity rights of survivorship payments
    D) joint life annuity payments

113. When may a firm sell a hot issue to its employee?
    A) when the firm is not an underwriter
    B) if the employee is not a registered representative
    C) only if the hot issue is the stock of the firm
    D) under no circumstances

114. Which of the following is the LOWEST investment-grade bond rating?
    A) AA
    B) BBB
    C) A
    D) C

115. Which of the following occurs upon annuitization of a variable annuity contract?
    A) The accumulation units value is used to determine the value of the annuity units.
    B) The accumulation units value is used to determine the number of annuity units.
    C) Separate account securities become taxable.
    D) Separate account securities are liquidated.

116. EFG stock is currently trading at $777. Which of the following customer trades, executed 2 weeks after the customer sold 100 shares of EFG stock, would result in a wash sale?
    A) The customer buys 1 EFG 770 put.
    B) The customer sells 1 EFG 800 call.
    C) The customer sells 1 EFG 870 put.
    D) The customer executes a short sale of 100 shares of EFG stock.

117. Which statement applies to warrants?
    A) Warrants generally have voting rights.
    B) Warrants are the same as short-term options.
    C) Warrants cover ten shares of the underlying stock.
    D) Warrants do not pay dividends.

118. Trades made in the third market are required to be reported on the Consolidated Tape within what period of time?
    A) 30 seconds
    B) 60 seconds
    C) 90 seconds
    D) 120 seconds

119. A city and a school district exist as coterminous entities, both with outstanding bond issues and drawing from the same taxpayers for debt support. This is an example of what type of debt?
    A) concentric
    B) contiguous
    C) direct
    D) overlapping

120. Who would execute an order from a member firm to buy 100 XYZ stock?
    A) registered representatives
    B) floor brokers
    C) specialists
    D) competitive traders

121. A trade of 10,000 shares that is announced on the tape after trade execution on the floor of an exchange is known as what type of trade?
    A) special offer
    B) secondary distribution
    C) specialist's bid
    D) exchange distribution

122. Which of the following entities guarantees a listed option contract?
    A) the Options Clearing Corp.
    B) broker-dealer firms
    C) the seller of the option
    D) the exchange where the option was traded

123. A group of investors is interested in the purchase of a new-issue municipal bond of Ironworks City. Where would the investors go for information about the issue?
    A) bond registration statement
    B) new issue prospectus
    C) preliminary official statement
    D) Moody's or S&P bond-rating service

124. What happens to municipal bonds that lose their tax-free status?
    A) Bond prices increase.
    B) Bond yields increase.
    C) Bond prices remain the same.
    D) Bond yields decrease.

125. Which of the following is NOT a responsibility of a designated market maker?
    A) to communicate with NYSE-listed companies to let them know how their stock is trading
    B) to provide liquidity to ease large market imbalances
    C) to oversee opening and closing auctions
    D) to approve floor brokers for trading of individual securities

126. Due to an unexpected special cash dividend of $0.88 for shareholders of HIJ stock, the Options Clearing Corp. (OCC) releases a note adjusting strikes for HIJ options. A holder of an HIJ May 44 call before the adjustment can expect to have his strike price adjusted to which of the following after the adjustment?
    A) $43.12
    B) $43.56
    C) $43.88
    D) $44.88

127. Assuming that both contracts are on the same strike and maturity, which of the following positions is a short straddle?
    A) long call, short put
    B) long call, long put
    C) short call, short put
    D) short call, long put

128. A customer enters an order for the purchase of XYZ stock at the best available price without specifying the price but expecting execution. What type of order is this?
    A) market order
    B) limit order
    C) stop order
    D) stop limit order

129. The purchase of a municipal bond at a premium results in a decrease in the book value of the bond during the period the bond is held. What is this process called?
    A) accretion
    B) accrual
    C) amortization
    D) depreciation

130. Investment advisers do NOT have to register with the SEC when the number of clients they work with during a 12-month period is fewer than how many?
    A) 10
    B) 15
    C) 20
    D) 25

131. A securities firm is the managing underwriter for an offering of Alameda County bonds. The bonds are to be sold to investors at par. Compensation will flow to members as follows: Syndicate nonmember broker-dealers will be able to purchase bonds at $990, and members of the underwriting syndicate may purchase bonds at $984. If syndicate member A purchases 100 bonds and sells them to a nonmember, what is the additional takedown?
    A) $6.00
    B) $9.00
    C) $15.00
    D) $24.00

132. Atlantic Railroad Corp. wants to sell 500,000 shares to the public. Of these, 200,000 are coming from the company's Treasury shares and 300,000 are new shares. What is this offering considered?
    A) initial public offering
    B) primary distribution
    C) secondary distribution
    D) split offering

133. What percent decline in the S&P 500 Index corresponds to a Level 3 market decline and automatically halts the New York Stock Exchange for the remainder of the trading day?
    A) 7%
    B) 10%
    C) 13%
    D) 20%

134. Which of the following statements is CORRECT concerning the purchase of open-end investment company shares?
    A) Registered representatives can receive continuing commissions for selling such shares after the termination of their employment with a FINRA member.
    B) A LOI for the purchase of shares is valid for a 24-month period after the initial transaction.
    C) The purchase of open-end investment company shares must be made before the payment of a declared dividend.
    D) Brokers are permitted to arrange for the extension of credit to a customer for the purchase of shares.

135. A municipality includes in its notice of sale for a new issue of bonds its preference for bidding syndicates to enter their bids based on true interest cost. Why would the municipality choose this method?
    A) The IRS prefers the true interest cost method.
    B) The true interest cost is easier to calculate.
    C) True interest cost is calculated using constant dollars.
    D) True interest cost is calculated using actual dollars.

Answer Key

1. **C)** Regulation D governs private placements.

2. **C)** An all-or-none underwriting would be canceled if all of the offering cannot be sold.

3. **B)** A specialist is permitted to accept a good-till-canceled (GTC) order.

4. **D)** This is an eastern account, or undivided account underwriting. Even though the dealer sold its allotment, it would be liable for 10% of the unsold allotment, or $300,000.

5. **A)** The notation cv stands for "convertible bond."

6. **D)** To purchase an option, the buyer must pay 100% of the premium.

7. **B)** Because the put option on XYZ expired worthless, the customer lost the entire $400 paid-in premium. As for the stock position, a $1,000 gain was made, resulting in a net profit of $600: $1,000 − $400 = $600.

8. **A)** Income from rents is the first revenue source for public housing revenue bonds.

9. **B)** The initial position was an opening purchase, and when the customer writes the same contract, it is a closing sale.

10. **C)** The purpose of purchasing the put is to protect the customer against a downside risk that the stock will lose market value. Holding the put allows the holder to "put" the stock to the writer at the strike price if the spot price of the underlying stock declines substantially.

11. **D)** The cost of the stock would be $55 + $4 for the call premium, resulting in an adjusted cost basis of $59 per share ($55 + $4 = $59).

12. **B)** To close out the position, the customer needs to purchase the same option contract. This results in $4,750 received less $2,125 paid: $4,750 − $2,125 = $2,625 net profit (before taxes).

13. **C)** Retained earnings are the component of net income that is not returned to shareholders (paid out as dividends, for example) but rather remains as a surplus. The percent of net income that is retained is called the retention ratio. It can be thought of as the proportion of net income that gets reinvested into the business instead of being distributed to the owners of the company.

14. **D)** The Options Clearing Corp. (OCC) places a 250,000 limit on the number of contracts that are permitted to be held on the same side of the market (bullish or bearish) in the same underlying security, with some exceptions for more heavily traded and/or diversified assets.

15. **B)** The depletion allowance for oil and gas limited partnerships is an advantage similar to depreciation in real estate. Limited partners are not involved in day-to-day management. General partners can have their personal assets seized to cover liabilities, including those that result from another general partner's actions.

16. **C)** The writer of the 10 calls received a total of $4,750 for the sale. If the price of the stock moves above $40.00, as long as it goes no higher than the strike price ($40.00) plus the premium received ($4.75), the customer profits. The initial price of the underlying stock is not a component of the break-even calculation.

17. **D)** The uncertainty of the company's fate due to the lawsuit makes the stock highly speculative and subject to a special situation that will influence its future price. Other special

situations include mergers and acquisitions (M&A) and pending regulatory approval (as for pharmaceutical companies waiting on FDA certification for a new drug). Substantial dislocations in price are more likely than usual, and the distribution of future prices may not be normal or symmetrical.

18. **A)** The call is in-the-money ($11 of intrinsic value), so it would be exercised and the put would expire worthless. This results in a gain of $1,100 for exercising the call minus a loss of $600 in total premium paid, for a net profit of $500: $1,100 - $600 = $500.

19. **C)** The breakeven for a long call spread is the strike price of the long call ($40) plus the debit ($3): $40 + $3 = $43.

20. **D)** Because municipal bonds are purchased in the secondary market at a discount to par, there is no adjustment (accretion) for the purchaser's cost. The gain on sale is the difference between the sale price ($1,030) less the original cost ($970): $1,030 - $970 = $60.

21. **D)** The combined premium received as a credit represents the maximum gain, which would typically be achieved only if the stock closes at $30 upon expiry. Incorporating the 100 multiplier, this results in a gain of $3,300 for exercising the call (30 + 3 = 33) and a loss of $2,500 on the put (30 - 5 = 25). $3,300 - $2,500 = $800.

22. **A)** US government securities issued with a maturity of 1 year or less are called Treasury bills. They are zero-coupon bonds. Treasury receipts are not issued by the US government.

23. **C)** Income stocks are generally derived from mature companies in stable industries.

24. **B)** The maximum potential loss for a put writer is the strike price less the premium received. Incorporating the 100 multiplier, $3,500 - 225 = $3,275.

25. **D)** Joint tenancy means that both parties must authorize transactions.

26. **A)** Common stock allows the shareholder to receive a pro rata share of dividends issued and vote for members of the board of directors.

27. **C)** $6.03 (public offering price) × 300 shares = $1,809, which includes the sales charge (SC) or commission.

28. **C)** Debentures are backed by the full faith and credit of the issuer.

29. **D)** A US government guarantee for Government National Mortgage Association (GNMA) securities ensures the timely payment of both principal and interest.

30. **B)** Inactive accounts receive statements on a quarterly basis unless there are options trades, in which case statements are sent monthly.

31. **C)** Under Regulation T, the margin requirement is 50% for convertible corporate bonds.

32. **A)** The difference between the ask and the bid for an over-the-counter (OTC) market maker is a price spread. As an issue becomes more active (heavily traded), the spread between ask-bid typically narrows.

33. **B)** To determine the parity price of the stock, take the par value of the bond and divide by price per share ($1,000 ÷ $50.00 = 20). Upon conversion, the customer will receive 20 shares of common stock. Take the market price of the convertible bond ($975) and divide by the number of shares into which the bond can be converted (20). $975 ÷ 20 = 48.75. The parity price equals $48.75.

34. **C)** A sinking fund holds money to pay debt or future capital expenses. Bondholders do not receive dividends. A sinking fund may be used to redeem bonds, repurchase bonds in the open market, or exercise a partial call.

35. **B)** A greenshoe permits the issuer to support the stock price immediately after an offering by oversubscribing the offering by up to 15%. If the stock price dips, shares for the oversubscribed portion can be bought at market, increasing the price elasticity of demand for the security.

Shares can never be lent out to short sellers before an IPO.

36. **B)** The net asset value (NAV), or bid, is the price received when redeeming shares of an open-end investment company.

37. **B)** The Trust Indenture Act of 1939 deals with the public offering of certain debt securities in more than one state or on an interstate basis.

38. **C)** Capitalization is the chief difference between open-end and closed-end investment companies. Open-end funds (referred to as mutual funds) continuously issue new shares for investors; closed-end funds (referred to as publicly traded funds) trade in the secondary market, similar to corporate stocks.

39. **D)** Income from a variable annuity will vary and is not fixed (as with a fixed annuity); this may be a concern for an individual who is dependent on a certain level of monthly income in retirement.

40. **B)** Market risk (also known as systematic risk) is the risk that a security may lose value due to a decline in the market.

41. **D)** Companies use a transfer agent and registrar to log ownership changes, generate and keep shareholder records, cancel and issue share certificates, make dividend distributions, and manage annual meeting services. These functions can be separated from one another, but in practice, they are often combined. Transfer agents must register with regulators.

42. **D)** The investment objectives of a mutual fund can take place with the approval of more than 50% of the fund's shareholders.

43. **B)** Preferred stock does not provide a guaranteed dividend; when dividends are issued and paid, they are based on a fixed (stated) rate.

44. **B)** According to the Investment Company Act of 1940, a 12b-1 fee is an annual marketing or distribution fee on a mutual fund.

45. **A)** The Bond Buyer 11 Bond Index, which consists of 11 of the 20 highest-rated general obligation (GO) municipal bonds found in the 20 Bond Index, has a lower yield.

46. **C)** The price per share that an investor receives upon redemption is the net asset value (NAV) less sales charge (SC) for the sales redemption price.

47. **D)** The customer must pay the execution price for the trade.

48. **C)** The pink sheets provide a list of stock prices held by market makers that are not listed on the NASDAQ.

49. **C)** Because there is an anti-dilution clause in the trust indenture, the conversion price of the stock would be reduced proportionately. The 10% stock dividend would be incorporated into the share price by increasing the conversion factor to 1.1 and dividing the conversion price of $25.00 for a new conversion price of $22.72.

50. **D)** The writer received $300 in premiums from the sale of the naked put (the maximum gain for a short option). But the writer lost $500 when ABC fell to $25 per share and the $30-strike contract was assigned (30 - 25 = 5; use the 100 multiplier for option contracts; 5 × 100 = 500). The net quantity is loss less profit: $500 - $300 = $200 loss.

51. **C)** Regulation T requires 50% initial equity for margined long stock positions. The total cost of the shares is $5,000, so the customer must have equity of $2,500 for this transaction.

52. **B)** The maximum gain for a bull put spread is the $400 premium collected by the customer when the position is opened. This gain will be realized if the options expire when the underlying price is above the higher strike price.

53. **C)** The Uniform Gifts to Minors Act is commonly known as UGMA. It allows custodial securities accounts to be established for minors.

54. **B)** Qualified private activity bonds are taxable under the alternative minimum tax. These bonds are issued by (or for) a municipal or state government to finance qualified projects, and they are typically exempt from many taxes.

55. **A)** The opening transactions for this call calendar position result in a net debit of $3. The closing transactions result in a net credit of $4. The overall profit or loss for this trade is a gain of $100.

56. **A)** The tangible net asset value (NAV) of a stock is the same as its book value.

57. **D)** More predictable cash flow is an advantage that collateralized mortgage obligations (CMOs) have over Government National Mortgage Association (GNMA) securities.

58. **C)** Customer securities at the time of a Securities Investor Protection Corp. (SIPC) liquidation are based on the prevailing market value at that time.

59. **B)** Long straddles are positions when a put and a call on the same underlying security are purchased with the same expiration and strike price. A long strangle involves a put strike that is lower than the call strike.

60. **D)** Rule 505 offerings may raise up to $5 million.

61. **A)** The life annuity payment option represents the largest potential payout to the holder of a variable annuity contract. It is calculated only on the life of the annuity's receiver.

62. **C)** Because investment-grade bonds are relatively safe from default (due to high credit ratings), the chief risk is the impact of inflation on the buying power of the bond's proceeds.

63. **B)** An analysis of the cash flow will provide information about the revenues and expenses of the limited partnership.

64. **C)** A long margin account can become restricted if it falls below the initial Regulation T requirement of 50% but remains above the minimum maintenance requirement of 25%.

65. **B)** In a long margin account, where the purchase is made, the long market value (LMV) is $18,000; a debit (DB) of 50% or $9,000, which is the Regulation T requirement, is created. Subtracting DB from LMV yields equity of $9,000. When the market value increases to $64 per share, the LMV rises to $19,200. Since it only takes $9,600 to meet Regulation T requirements, the excess $600 in equity created is credited to the special memorandum account (SMA). Once SMA is credited, it does not diminish unless the customer uses the balance. When the LMV of XYZ drops to $58 per share, the account value falls to $17,400. DB remains unchanged, and the equity falls by $1,800 to $8,400. SMA is unaffected at $600.

66. **C)** Corporate bonds, series EE bonds, and face-amount certificates are fixed-value investments that are susceptible to inflation risk. Variable annuity accumulation units fall and rise based on the performance of the securities held in the separate account, providing a better potential hedge against inflation.

67. **B)** A seller of a put is obligated to purchase the underlying stock at the strike price when a buyer elects to exercise the contract.

68. **A)** The parity price of the common stock can be determined by dividing the call price ($102) by the number of shares of common stock into which the preferred stock is convertible (4 shares), equaling $25.50 ($102 ÷ 4 = $25.50). Because the common stock is trading at $20.00 per share, the shareholder should allow the preferred stock to be called, resulting in four shares valued higher than the prevailing market value.

69. **B)** The breakeven for a short put is the strike price ($30) minus the premium received ($3), which equals $27 ($30 − $3 = $27).

70. **B)** Municipal bonds settle in 2 days (T + 2).

71. **B)** The offering price is higher than the net asset value (NAV), so Options C and D must be incorrect. To determine the offering price, take the NAV and divide it by 100% minus the sales load percentage:

    $16.50 ÷ (100.0% − 8.0%)
    = $16.50 ÷ (92.0%)
    = $16.50 ÷ 0.92
    = $17.93

    The correct answer is 92.0%.

72. **D)** The maximum loss for a long straddle is the combined premiums paid ($400/call + $200/put = $600).

73. **D)** The position is a short straddle. The price of ABC fell to $19, the put was assigned, and the call expired worthless. The writer of the put will purchase 100 shares of stock for $30 per share ($3,000) despite its market value being $19 ($1,900), resulting in a loss of $1,100. Premiums of $8 ($800) were received up front by the writer of the put, so the net loss is $300 ($1,100 – $800 = $300).

74. **C)** The ABC Jul 40 call expires worthless, so the only potential economic gain from this call calendar comes from the ABC Nov 40 call. If the price of the stock goes to $43 (after the expiration of the Jul 40 call), the holder may exercise the ABC Nov 40 call and sell his shares to recoup his initial net premium debit of $300.

75. **C)** The fair market value is used to determine whether the gift must be reported to the IRS by the giver, but it is not the cost basis. The giver can give up to $15,000 in gifts per recipient per year without reporting the gifts on a tax return, and gifts with a value beyond $15,000 are not taxed until they exceed the lifetime exclusion ($11.58 million for 2020, raised to $11.7 million for 2021). Although the recipient pays nothing for the shares he receives, his cost basis is not zero; rather, the giver's cost basis is transferred to the recipient and will be used to determine capital gain (or loss) when the recipient sells the stock.

76. **B)** The registered representative has engaged in the sale of a security without the broker-dealer's permission, which is known as "selling away" and violates FINRA rules.

77. **C)** Unless otherwise specified, trades in a variety of securities settle based on a regular-way settlement, which is 2 business days after the trade date.

78. **C)** More than a year after the purchase date, the investor sold his shares at $40 per share. The sale price of the stock is $10 lower than what he paid per share; thus, the investor incurs a long-term capital loss on 100 shares at $10 per share.

79. **D)** The bond interest payments are based on par value, which is $1,100. Because interest payments for corporate bonds are made on a semiannual basis, the payment will be $110 (10% of $1,100).

80. **A)** All-cash deals tend to reduce volatility (standard deviation) of the target company's shares the most because the price of the stock typically stabilizes slightly below the deal price. In contrast, all-stock deals inherit volatility from the acquirer company's shares. Cash-and-stock deals fall somewhere in the middle. Acquisitions can be troublesome for holders of long-dated call options on the target company's shares because option's implied volatility tends to drop precipitously when an all-cash deal is announced.

81. **D)** Prior preferred stock (also called preference stock) is given priority for dividends and in liquidation order over common and preferred stock.

82. **C)** This strategy is a bull put spread. It incurs a credit because the long put is purchased for $4, and the short put is sold at $8 ($8 – $4 = $4). The difference between the strike prices ($85 – $75 = $10) minus the credit equals the maximum loss: $10 – $4 = $6. Using the 100 multiplier, the maximum loss is $600.

83. **B)** States establish blue sky laws. They are separate from, but similar to, federal securities laws insofar as they protect investors from fraudulent exploitation in the securities markets. The term refers to a quote from Supreme Court Justice Joseph McKenna about "speculative schemes which have no more basis than so many feet of blue sky."

84. **B)** Regulation T mandates that investors may borrow up to 50% of the initial cost of stocks that can be purchased on margin. FINRA supplements Regulation T's requirements by mandating that maintenance margin not fall below 25%.

85. **C)** Unit investment trusts (UITs) are unmanaged trusts that invest in a fixed portfolio. UITs do not need active management (hence, no management fee) because the trust exercises

no discretion in the composition of its assets. The other options (A, B, and D) require a greater degree of management and allow greater freedom to alter and rebalance the composition of their investments.

86. **D)** The management and advisory fees for a money market fund are often the largest operating expense.

87. **C)** Illustrated rates of return in sales literature for variable life insurance explain to customers how their death benefits and cash value may be affected.

88. **B)** Regulation T deals with the extension of margin credit from broker-dealers and their customers. Regulation G was established to provide transparency regarding a bank's compliance with anti-discrimination lending laws. Regulation D pertains to private placement exemptions. Regulation X protects consumers applying for and securing mortgage loans.

89. **B)** Whenever an investor buys a municipal bond at a premium, the premium must be amortized.

90. **D)** A change in interest rates will affect the price of long-term bonds more than short-term bonds. The bonds maturing in 10 years will have the greatest price change, as they have the longest-term maturity.

91. **C)** The breakeven for a long call is the strike price plus the premium paid ($25 + $3 = $28).

92. **B)** Individuals participating in an employer-sponsored qualified retirement plan may also contribute to an individual retirement account (either traditional or Roth IRA) under the provisions of the Tax Reform Act of 1986. Depending on their income level, they may be able to deduct contributions to a traditional IRA from gross income.

93. **A)** Fixed-maturity securities, also known as fixed-income securities, provide a known, fixed, periodic payment. At maturity, they return the principal. Bonds are the most common type of fixed-income securities; however, preferred stocks can also be fixed-income securities. Certificates of deposit (CDs) and money markets are other types of fixed-income securities.

94. **C)** Price has an inverse relationship to yield. When the customer purchased the bond, the yield to maturity was greater than the coupon rate, meaning the bond was purchased at a discount to par. When the customer sold the bond, the yield to maturity was less than the nominal yield, meaning the bond is trading above par or at a premium. Because the customer purchased the bond at a discount and sold it at a premium, there would be a gain on the transaction.

95. **B)** If the customer can purchase rights, the stock is trading ex-rights and the market price is adjusted for the value of the rights. One right in this offering is presently worth a fair value of $0.67 ([$45.00 - $43.00] ÷ 3 = $0.67). Because the rights are trading for more than this value, the market price of the stock must go to $45.25 or higher for the rights to be profitable as priced in the market.

96. **D)** This situation describes a discretionary transaction. According to FINRA Rule 3260, it requires written authorization from the customer and approval by the registered representative's firm.

97. **A)** The call is assigned when it is 15 points in-the-money. As a result, the writer will sell ABC stock for $30 per share ($3,000) when it is worth $45 per share ($4,500), resulting in a loss of $1,500 (using the 100 multiplier for listed contracts, $4,500 - $3,000 = $1,500). Premiums of $8 ($800) were received as a credit, so the customer's net loss is $700, and the put expires worthless.

98. **D)** Millage, or mill rate, is used by some institutions to determine property tax liability. A mill is 1/1,000 of a dollar, so the mill rate is equal to 0.001 per dollar. In terms of the property tax liability owed, 5 mills would mean the tax rate is 0.005 per dollar. The calculation is: $1,000,000 × 0.005 = $5,000.

99. **A)** The investor has held this position continuously for over a year, so she must pay long-term capital gains tax on the profits. Her

net gain is $2.60, and the relevant tax rate is 20%, so she owes $52.00.

100. **C)** The maximum profit for the holder of a put is the strike price less the premium paid. Using the 100 multiplier, $3,000 - $300 = $2,700.

101. **D)** Backing away is a prohibited practice whereby market makers do not honor their quoted bids and offers. The market maker has backed away from his firm offer of $15.46 for the stock by failing to execute the customer's limit order. Interpositioning is a deceptive and illegal practice of using a third party to generate extra commissions; hypothecation is involved in lending, so it is irrelevant here; and disintermediation essentially means "cutting out the middleman" in transactions or decision-making processes.

102. **C)** An increase in the share price of an open-end investment, like a US mutual fund, is referred to as a "price appreciation." Capital appreciation is often a stated goal for mutual funds, and it does not turn into a capital gain until a taxable event occurs.

103. **C)** Treasury bonds have a maturity of more than 10 years and provide interest coupon payments. The other options either have shorter maturity rates or do not have coupons attached. Treasury bills are short term with a maturity of 1 year or less; Treasury notes have a maturity between 1 and 10 years. Treasury receipts are a zero-coupon bond, meaning the investor buys the receipt at a deep discount and, when the bond reaches maturity, can receive the full value of the receipt.

104. **B)** The dividend is explicitly stated as a $6 sum rather than as a yield, which means that no par value is necessary to determine the dividend payout.

105. **C)** In a long margin account, where the purchase is made, the long market value (LMV) is $10,000. A debit (DB) of 50% or $5,000, which is the Regulation T requirement, is created. Subtracting DB from LMV yields equity of $5,000 ($10,000 - $5,000 = $5,000).

When the market value of the convertible bonds increases to 110, the LMV rises to $11,000. Because only $5,500 is needed to meet Regulation T requirements, an excess equity of $500 is created: $11,000 - $5,500 = $5,500; $5,500 - $5,000 = $500). The excess equity is credited to the special memorandum account (SMA).

106. **B)** A state requires that a certificate of limited partnership be filed to establish a limited partnership.

107. **B)** Fees to a firm's customers must be fair and reasonable and not unfairly discriminatory among its customers.

108. **D)** Instinet is an agency-only over-the-counter (OTC) trading system for private institutions. These trades occur in the fourth market, without a traditional intermediary that charges brokerage fees.

109. **A)** Collateralized mortgage obligations (CMOs) with three sequential tranches pay off principal and stop paying interest tranche A, then tranche B, then tranche C. The highest contraction (prepayment) risk belongs to tranche A, and the highest extension (late payoff) risk belongs to tranche C. Tranche Z would receive no cash payments until the preceding tranches are retired.

110. **C)** Depending on whether the investor lives in the municipality issuing the bonds, the interest income on the bonds can be tax exempt at the city (municipal), state, and federal levels.

111. **C)** Pattern day traders may trade up to four times their maintenance margin excess, but they must maintain a minimum account equity of $25,000 on any day that they trade.

112. **D)** The joint life annuity payment option ensures that payments will continue to the survivor upon the death of the first tenant (typically a spouse).

113. **C)** Firms are permitted to sell hot issues of their securities to their employees.

114. **B)** Bonds that are deemed investment grade have ratings of AAA, AA, A, or BBB. Bonds that are rated C or lower are considered high-yield bonds, or junk bonds.

115. **B)** A fixed number of annuity units will be received by the annuitant based on the value of the accumulation units upon annuitization.

116. **C)** A wash sale occurs when a customer closes one position and opens a substantially identical one within the 30 days before or after the trade date. Option A is incorrect because buying a put has opposite directional exposure (bearish) to the shares that were held previously (bullish), so it is not substantially identical. Option B is also incorrect for the same reason; short calls increase in value as the stock declines. Option C is correct because the profit profile of a deep in-the-money put behaves very similarly to 100 shares of stock. Option D is incorrect because short stock is not substantially identical to long stock.

117. **D)** Warrants represent a right, but not an obligation, to purchase shares of the underlying stock directly from the issuer. Until the warrant is exercised, the stock has not been bought, so there are no dividends paid to the warrant holder. Warrants are often structured like options, but they generally have a longer time to maturity. The number of shares addressed by each warrant can vary; an investor may need several warrants to purchase one share.

118. **C)** In accordance with FINRA rules, third market trades must be reported within 90 seconds.

119. **D)** Coterminous entities share the same taxing boundaries. Because such entities rely on the same revenue sources (taxpayers) to service their respective debts, this would be overlapping debt.

120. **B)** A floor broker performs order executions for member firms.

121. **D)** A large trade of 10,000 shares or more reported on the tape as a block after trade completion is an exchange distribution.

122. **A)** Listed options contracts are cleared and guaranteed by the Options Clearing Corporation (OCC).

123. **C)** The bond's official statement would provide investors with information about a new-issue municipal bond, just as a prospectus provides information about a new-issue corporate security. Municipal bonds are exempt from the registration requirements under the Securities Act of 1933.

124. **B)** Municipal bonds that lose their tax-free status are less valuable than identical bonds that have tax-free status. A drop in bond prices corresponds to an increase in bond yields.

125. **D)** Designated market makers, formerly called specialists, assume accountability for orderly trading of stocks on the NYSE. They serve as liaisons to issuers listed on the exchange, provide liquidity to offset imbalances, reinforce the National Best Bid and Offer (NBBO) throughout the trading day, oversee the opening and closing auctions, facilitate price discovery, and dampen volatility. They are not, however, responsible for the approval of floor brokers; that is a responsibility that belongs to the exchange itself.

126. **A)** Strikes for non-negligible special cash distributions are typically adjusted down by the amount of the distribution. This is done to compensate for an unexpected reduction in the forward price, upon which the option is priced. $44.00 − $0.88 = $43.12.

127. **C)** The sale of a call and put on the same security with the same strike price and expiration date is called a short straddle. It is a neutral position for a market that is moving sideways where the customer is looking to profit from the premiums received.

128. **A)** Market orders are the only type of order that guarantees immediate execution. Market orders may trade at a price that is substantially higher or lower than the last trade.

129. **C)** The cost of the bond's premium is being amortized over the holding period.

130. **B)** Under the provisions of the Investment Advisers Act of 1940, a person who gives investment advice for a fee to more than fifteen persons is required to register with the SEC as an investment adviser.

131. A) The syndicate member would receive $16.00 for her purchase ($1,000 − $984 = $16.00) and give back the difference between the selling and the concession received ($1,000 − $990 = $10.00; $16.00 − $10.00 = $6.00).

132. D) The offering described is a split offering, also known as a combined offering, because it includes a primary distribution of new shares and a secondary distribution of previously issued Treasury shares.

133. D) Per NYSE Rule 7.12, the enumerated levels of market decline are 7%, 13%, and 20%. At a 7% or 13% decline (once each per day), trading is halted for 15 minutes as long as more than 35 minutes remain in the trading day. At a 20% decline (regardless of the time of day), the exchange will halt trading in all stocks for the rest of the day.

134. A) FINRA Rule 2040 stipulates that, under a written agreement with a member firm, registered representatives can receive continuing commissions for selling mutual fund shares even after their employment ends with the member, so Option A is correct. An investor's purchase of additional shares of a fund in order to qualify for a quantity discount (breakpoint) must take place within 13 months after a letter of intent (LOI) is signed. Selling dividends is an unfair trade practice, and mutual funds are not eligible as marginable securities.

135. C) True interest cost is calculated using constant dollars, which account for the net present value of interest payments made to investors. In other words, true interest cost is more transparent than alternative methods for computing the cost of a loan because it explicitly expresses the time value of money.

4 Practice Test 4

1. An associated person writes a retail communication recommending LMN stock as an attractive buy at $2.20. Three months later, LMN stock trades at an all-time high of $55.95. In what case may the associated person write follow-up correspondence that lists this extremely profitable recommendation without mentioning any other past recommendations?

   A) This is always permitted.
   B) This is permitted only if the firm has made no other recommendation for similar securities in the past year.
   C) This is permitted only if the firm has made no other recommendations in the past year at all.
   D) This is never permitted.

2. WXY Beverage Corp. has filed for Chapter 7 bankruptcy and is closing its operations permanently. WXY's liquidation proceeds are insufficient to cover its debt burden. What is the net loss incurred by a trader who is short 3 WXY Sep 45 puts if he sold them at $3.50 when WXY was trading at $50.00?

   A) $12,450
   B) $13,500
   C) $13,950
   D) $14,550

3. When can a FINRA member firm sell collateralized mortgage obligations (CMOs) to a first-time customer without providing educational materials about CMO characteristics and risks?

   A) never
   B) when the customer affirms in writing that she understands CMOs and their risks
   C) when the customer is an institutional investor
   D) any time

4. A block of 300,000 shares of DEF stock changes hands in a single transaction on a dark pool. When is the dark pool required to report this transaction to FINRA?

   A) within 10 seconds
   B) within 15 minutes
   C) before 8:00 p.m. EST
   D) never

5. When is a member permitted to temporarily prevent disbursements from an account in good standing that belongs to an adult customer believed to have no mental or physical impairment?

   A) when the customer is 65 or older
   B) under no circumstances
   C) upon reasonable belief that exploitation has happened, will happen, or is happening
   D) when A and C are both true

6. Which of the following constitutes backing away by a member firm?
   A) placing an offer to tighten a market, then canceling it and buying from other offers at that price
   B) providing a firm quotation to a customer and then refusing to trade promptly at that level
   C) buying and selling a large amount of the same penny stock to create an illusion of activity
   D) trading for a principal account before effecting a same-way agency transaction for a customer

7. A broker-dealer establishes a monthly list of trade recommendations based on extensive analysis of risk and reward and sends them only to retail customers whose specific investment profiles and risk appetites are a match for all of the recommended trades. One of those customers receives the list and asks if he should trade all of the recommendations simultaneously in his portfolio. Based on the suitability standard, is there a reason for the broker-dealer to recommend against this course of action?
   A) No; customers bear the burden of determining the suitability of a recommendation.
   B) No; the suitability of each recommendation is considered separate from other recommendations.
   C) Yes; all of the individual recommendations may be good, but they may be dangerously correlated.
   D) Yes; a customer should never trade every recommendation provided by a broker-dealer.

8. Which of the following is used to establish whether a firm is considered a "taping firm"?
   A) gross notional transaction volume effected annually
   B) disciplinary history of associated persons
   C) FOMC commentary indicating a scale-down of bond buying
   D) case-by-case discretion by FINRA's board of governors

9. A customer has been analyzing PQR stock for several months. She is bullish, but the recent earnings print was very bad and PQR stock has dropped by 20% in the past 2 weeks. The customer decides to take a 3-month option position that would profit both from an appreciation in PQR stock and a reduction in the implied volatility of PQR options. Which of the following trades would BEST express the customer's view? (Assume that today is March 15 and PQR stock is presently trading at $70.)
   A) opening sale of a PQR Jun 70 put
   B) opening buy of a PQR Jun 70 call
   C) buy a PQR Jun 65/70 put spread
   D) sell a PQR Jun 70/75 call spread

10. A customer submits a limit bid of $40.50 for 30,000 shares of NOP stock. His floor broker on the NYSE quickly executes a buy of 20,000 shares for $40.50, but the stock rallies and the balance of 10,000 shares goes unfilled. The broker erroneously gives the customer an execution report describing a buy of 30,000 shares of NOP for $40.50. Later in the day, after NOP closes at $43.50, the broker identifies the error, contacts the customer, and sends a corrected execution report. The customer demands to be filled on all 30,000 shares for $40.50 or have the trade canceled entirely. What trade will the customer know?
    A) buy of 20,000 NOP for $40.50
    B) buy of 30,000 NOP for $40.50
    C) buy of 30,000 NOP for an average price of $41.50
    D) nothing done on the day

11. A member firm files Form U4 to register a new hire as an associated person, but the member is unable to review a copy of the new hire's most recent Form U5. What must the member do if it is unable to review Form U5 within 60 days of filing Form U4?
    A) No additional action is required.
    B) The member must demonstrate to FINRA that it took steps to review the most recent Form U5.
    C) The member must withdraw the Form U4 filing until it can review the most recent Form U5.
    D) The member must terminate the employment of the new hire.

12. Which of the following positions makes the most sense for a customer who believes that DEF stock, which pays no dividends, will close at exactly $30 on Jan options expiry 6 months from now?

    A) long DEF Jan 20/30/40 call butterfly spread
    B) long DEF Jan 10/20/30 call butterfly spread
    C) short DEF Jan 20/30/40 put butterfly spread
    D) short DEF Jan 15/25/35 put butterfly spread

13. A registered representative in New York City is prohibited from cold-calling a prospective customer's residence at 10:30 a.m. EST if that customer

    A) has not specifically requested a cold call.
    B) has published their phone number in a public directory.
    C) resides in San Francisco, California.
    D) is not listed in the FTC's do-not-call registry.

14. A customer effects a buy-write by purchasing 100 shares of ABC stock for $38.00 per share and selling 1 ABC May 40 call option at $2.40. What is her break-even price in ABC?

    A) $35.60
    B) $37.60
    C) $40.40
    D) $42.40

15. Firm X is a member of a selling group, and Firm Y is not a participant in the offering. Firm X sells a small number of shares to Firm Y at a price that is slightly below the public offering price. This is considered to be what?

    A) illegal
    B) reallowance
    C) retention
    D) undercutting

16. An investor buys and holds YZ stock. She says that she made this investment because the dividend yield of YZ is high, and its share price has historically been stable. Which of the following BEST describes the investor's motive?

    A) growth
    B) income
    C) arbitrage
    D) speculation

17. An investor with no other positions sells a STU Feb 200-strike put at a premium of $15. Upon Feb expiration, the stock closes at $190 and he is assigned 100 shares. What is the per-share cost basis of his long STU position after assignment? (Assume no commissions.)

    A) $185
    B) $190
    C) $200
    D) $205

18. Which of the following bonds would show yield to call on the trade confirmation?

    A) 10% nominal yield, 12% yield to maturity
    B) 10% nominal yield, 10% yield to maturity
    C) 10% nominal yield, 8% yield to maturity
    D) 10% nominal yield, 14% yield to maturity

19. The approval of municipal securities advertisement is performed by

    A) the MSRB.
    B) the NYSE.
    C) the principal.
    D) the SEC.

20. Which of the following is necessarily true of a Treasury note that trades roughly at par?

    A) Its current yield roughly equals its nominal yield.
    B) Its nominal yield roughly equals zero.
    C) Its current yield roughly equals zero.
    D) It is an on-the-run Treasury security.

21. Which of the following methods for holding securities allows investors to maintain stock ownership in book entry form with the issuer?

    A) physical certificates
    B) direct registration
    C) street-name registration
    D) Treasury stock

22. When may customers trade a subject offer they receive from a broker-dealer?

    A) always
    B) never
    C) within 60 seconds of receiving the quotation
    D) at the discretion of the broker-dealer

23. An investor short-sells a 100-strike LEAPS put option on the stock of ABCD Corp., expiring 3 years from the date of sale, at $30. Two years later, the investor covers the put for $4. How is this trade taxed? (Assume the investor has no other positions in any security.)
    A) long-term capital gains on $2,600 profit
    B) long-term capital gains on $26,000 profit
    C) short-term capital gains on $2,600 profit
    D) short-term capital gains on $26,000 profit

24. The common stock of HIJK Robotics Corp. comes in two classes: HIJK shares that lack shareholder voting rights and HIJKL shares that allow one shareholder vote per share. In all other respects, including dividends and capital structure priority, the share classes are identical. The only qualitative difference between HIJK shares and HIJKL shares stems from voting rights. Which, if either, of the two share classes will trade cheaper in the market?
    A) HIJK and HIJKL will trade at the same price.
    B) HIJK can be expected to trade cheaper than HIJKL.
    C) HIJKL can be expected to trade cheaper than HIJK.
    D) Not enough information is provided.

25. Of the following account types, which may a broker liquidate due to a decline in market value?
    A) cash
    B) margin
    C) traditional IRA
    D) Roth IRA

26. Under what circumstances may a variable annuity be represented in a member's marketing communications as a short-term, liquid investment?
    A) only when administrative fees are not charged
    B) only when marketed to adults over age 65
    C) under no circumstances
    D) at the discretion of the member

27. A trader sold 2 SPY Apr 400 puts at the Chicago Board of Exchange on a Tuesday. When will this transaction settle?
    A) Tuesday
    B) Wednesday
    C) Thursday
    D) Friday

28. In the recent fiscal year, VWX Animation reported earnings per share of $12 and a net profit margin of 48%. VWX stock closed today at $600. Based on this information, what is the P/E ratio of VWX?
    A) 0.48
    B) 4
    C) 12.5
    D) 50

29. Which of the following scenarios is defined by FINRA as "clearly erroneous"? (Assume that each scenario takes place during normal market hours—9:30 a.m. to 4:00 p.m. EST.)
    A) ABC Airlines stock is halted due to impending news about a crash and resumes trading 7% lower.
    B) A nervous trader accidentally pays $28 for DEF stock, which traded at $26 immediately prior.
    C) The chief executive of GHIJ & Sons is indicted for embezzlement, and GHIJ stock drops by 20%.
    D) An anxious trader accidentally pays $23 for KL stock, which traded at $21 immediately prior.

30. A registered representative is the only trader of PQR stock in an independent trading unit of a member firm that qualifies for independent trading unit aggregation. Her account holds a long position of 20,000 PQR shares. Her firm has a net short position of 100,000 PQR shares. The registered representative will sell 10,000 shares of PQR stock to hedge an existing position today. How should she mark this order ticket?
    A) long sale
    B) short sale
    C) short-exempt sale
    D) long-exempt sale

31. Select the option strategy that can be described as a straddle.
    A) long XYZ Jan 20 put and long XYZ Jan 25 call
    B) long XYZ Jan 20 put and short XYZ Feb 20 put
    C) long XYZ Jan 20 put and long XYZ Jan 20 call
    D) long XYZ Jan 20 put and short XYZ Jan 25 call

32. A European-style Sep option can be exercised on Sep option expiration. When can an American-style Sep option be exercised?
    A) Aug option expiration
    B) Sep option expiration
    C) Oct option expiration
    D) both A and B

33. Which of the following debt products is NOT secured with collateral?
    A) equipment trust certificate
    B) senior debenture
    C) residential mortgage-backed security
    D) credit card asset–backed security

34. Which of the following bonds is MOST likely to be included in the Bond Buyer Index?
    A) a corporate bond with 40 years remaining until maturity
    B) a corporate bond with 20 years remaining until maturity
    C) a municipal bond with 20 years remaining until maturity
    D) a municipal bond with 11 years remaining until maturity

35. Which of the following investments can be expected to cost the LEAST?
    A) $1 million of notional in a high-yield bond with 5 years to maturity and a 2% coupon
    B) $1 million of notional in an investment-grade bond with 5 years to maturity and a 2% coupon
    C) $1 million of notional in a Treasury bond trading at par with a 2% coupon
    D) $1 million of notional in a Treasury note with 5 years to maturity and a 2% coupon

36. MNO stock is trading at $16.25, and the MNO Nov 18 put is offered at $3.20. What is the intrinsic value of the MNO Nov 18 put?
    A) $0
    B) $1.45
    C) $1.75
    D) $3.20

37. Select the true statement.
    A) Hedge funds are not subject to any disclosure requirements.
    B) Hedge funds are subject to more stringent disclosure requirements than mutual funds.
    C) Hedge funds are subject to the same disclosure requirements as mutual funds.
    D) Hedge funds are subject to less stringent disclosure requirements than mutual funds.

38. Why might a 12b-1 fee be charged from the assets of a mutual fund?
    A) back-end sales load
    B) mailings to prospective investors
    C) payroll for employees of the mutual fund company
    D) office space for business operations

39. At what stage of a complaint can a FINRA member engage in mediation with a customer?
    A) before filing a claim for arbitration
    B) after filing a claim for arbitration
    C) after arbitration dates have been scheduled
    D) all of the above

40. An investor buys 1 SPX Apr 4,500 call for $240.50 and sells 1 SPX Jul 4,500 call at $300.50. On the morning of Apr expiration, the exercise-settlement value is $3,862.10. On the morning of Jul expiration, the exercise-settlement value is $4,810.50. Assuming no other trades were executed, what is the investor's profit or loss?
    A) gain of $6,000
    B) gain of $57,790
    C) loss of $25,050
    D) loss of $57,790

41. All else being equal, which of the following types of municipal bonds issued by the City of Smallton is backed by the full faith and credit of Smallton?

    A) general obligation bond to build a schoolhouse in West Smallton
    B) revenue bond to build an Olympic-sized swimming pool in North Smallton
    C) moral obligation bond to buy salt trucks and snowplows for areas near Mount Smallton
    D) none of the above

42. On the first trading day of a new year, a speculator bought the FGH 300 call option expiring in January of the following year. He paid a premium of $40 for this LEAPS option. On expiration day over a year later, he closed the option at intrinsic value versus a stock price of $390. How will he be taxed on the gain from this transaction?

    A) long-term capital gains tax on a profit of $5,000
    B) long-term capital gains tax on a profit of $9,000
    C) short-term capital gains tax on a profit of $5,000
    D) short-term capital gains tax on a profit of $9,000

43. Which of the following equity securities constitutes an American depositary receipt (ADR)?

    A) LMNO, a Brazilian issuance for a commercial meatpacking business
    B) PQRS, a US issuance for a US-based importer of industrial equipment
    C) TUVW, a US issuance representing Taiwan-listed stock in a computer chip manufacturer
    D) XYZ, a US listing for a Chinese internet commerce company

44. In general, which of the following securities is most susceptible to duration extension risk?

    A) common stock listed on the NYSE
    B) 30-year US Treasury bonds
    C) corporate debentures with no call or put provisions
    D) pass-through RMBS

45. EFG Company reported a disappointing quarterly earnings number this morning: its stock has stabilized at $33.95 after falling 12% in a volatile trading session. What is the time value of the Aug 33 put, if its premium is $6.85?

    A) $0
    B) $0.95
    C) $5.90
    D) $6.85

46. A Treasury note auction receives four competitive bids at the following yields, with each bid exactly equal in size to one-third of the total auction offering. Not a single noncompetitive bid is placed. Which competitive bid determines the coupon rate of the Treasury note?

    A) 1.43%
    B) 1.56%
    C) 1.64%
    D) 1.65%

47. When can a member firm send retail communications about investment company rankings based on total returns for a time period of less than 1 year?

    A) never
    B) only for money market mutual funds
    C) only for closed-end funds that invest in US-listed equities
    D) only for UITs that invest in Treasury bonds

48. What is the term for the threshold dollar amount beyond which a mutual fund investor pays a discounted front-end sales load?

    A) gross point
    B) inflection point
    C) breakpoint
    D) strike price

49. A Section 1256 option was bought in June and sold 6 months later. How is the profit taxed?

    A) 100% as long-term capital gains
    B) 100% as short-term capital gains
    C) 50% as long-term capital gains and 50% as short-term capital gains
    D) 60% as long-term capital gains and 40% as short-term capital gains

50. According to Regulation FD, an issuer who discloses material nonpublic information to a stock analyst who works for a particular investment bank must also disclose that information to whom?

   A) the Securities and Exchange Commission
   B) the public
   C) stock analysts at other investment banks
   D) shareholders

51. Which of the following is NOT considered a qualified transfer of funds and might thus be subject to the gift tax?

   A) a grandparent directly paying a granddaughter's tuition at the local university
   B) a granddaughter directly paying a grandparent's tuition at the local university
   C) a granddaughter directly paying a grandparent's utility bill to a municipality
   D) a grandparent directly paying a granddaughter's hospital bill for an appendectomy

52. In an inflationary environment, which of the following accounting methods would reflect the largest tax liability for a company that manufactures and sells a single model of lawn tractor?

   A) first-in-first-out
   B) last-in-first-out
   C) average cost
   D) no difference

53. A customer owns 200 shares of CDEF stock, purchased for an average price of $20.20. She sells a 21-strike call expiring in June to collect a premium of $0.50. At Jun expiry, that call is assigned and she subsequently sells a 22-strike call expiring in November to collect a premium of $0.40. The closing price of CDEF on Nov expiry is $25.00, and the Nov call is assigned. What is the customer's total profit from her CDEF options and stock?

   A) $75
   B) $180
   C) $260
   D) $335

54. Which of the following debt securities, all paying a 2.0% semiannual coupon, has the highest clean price? (Assume a current yield of 2.1% for the 30-year benchmark Treasury bond, a current yield of 1.7% for the 10-year benchmark Treasury note, and no call provisions.)

   A) corporate bond maturing in 30 years, offered at a yield spread of +50 basis points
   B) corporate bond maturing in 30 years, offered at a yield spread of +100 basis points
   C) corporate bond maturing in 10 years, offered at a yield spread of +100 basis points
   D) corporate bond maturing in 10 years, offered at a yield spread of +150 basis points

55. EFG Corp. will report quarterly earnings on the morning of Jan options expiry. An investor owns 400,000 shares of EFG stock, currently trading at $34.00. He holds no other securities. The investor is confident about the long-term outlook for EFG Corp., but he fears that EFG stock will trade down sharply if quarterly sales fall short of expectations. Which of the following options trades would BEST protect the investor's stock position if EFG falls to $32.00 on earnings day?

   A) sell 4,000 EFG Jan 34 put at $0.25
   B) sell 4,000 EFG Jan 34 call at $0.25
   C) buy 4,000 EFG Jan 34 put for $0.25
   D) buy 4,000 EFG Jan 34 call for $0.25

56. A trader sells 2 XYZ Jun 35 calls and buys 1 XYZ Jun 30 straddle. She collects a premium of $1.20 for each Jun 35 call and pays $4.00 in premium for the Jun 30 straddle. She has no other positions. Which of the following is a break-even level, in terms of the price of XYZ stock?

   A) $28.40
   B) $30.00
   C) $31.40
   D) $35.80

57. A young trader sells 3 cash-secured Jan 30 puts on OPQ stock at $10 each on the Chicago Board of Exchange. What is the maximum potential loss associated with this trade?

   A) $2,990
   B) $3,000
   C) $6,000
   D) $8,700

58. Where may a Regulation S debt security trade?
    A) within the issuer's state of incorporation
    B) outside of the United States
    C) at a national market system exchange
    D) anywhere, but only between FINRA member firms

59. According to the capital asset pricing model (CAPM), how does an increase in the risk-free rate affect the expected return of an asset with a beta of zero?
    A) There is an increase in the expected return for the asset.
    B) There is a decrease in the expected return for the asset.
    C) There is no change in the expected return for the asset.
    D) There is not enough information provided.

60. Which of the following is usually exempt from federal tax?
    A) corporate bond interest income
    B) profits from the sale of a corporate bond
    C) municipal bond interest income
    D) profits from the sale of a municipal bond

61. Which of the following corporate actions would justify the early exercise of a deep in-the-money listed US equity call option on Monday, January 5? The call option expires in March and its time value is $0.50 at the close of trading on January 5.
    A) a regular cash dividend of $2.50 with a record date of Tuesday, January 6
    B) a regular cash dividend of $2.50 with a record date of Wednesday, January 7
    C) a 2-for-1 stock split with a record date of Tuesday, January 6
    D) a 2-for-1 stock split with a record date of Wednesday, January 7

62. Nonqualified dividends are typically taxed as what?
    A) ordinary income
    B) corporate income
    C) long-term capital gains
    D) short-term capital gains

63. In which case is a brokerage NOT required to send a quarterly statement for a retail account?
    A) The retail account has no holdings during the quarter.
    B) The retail account has no transactions during the quarter.
    C) The retail account has no entry, money, or security position during the preceding quarter.
    D) The retail account has no transactions or holdings during the preceding quarter.

64. A collateralized mortgage obligation has a single prepayment speed assumption and protects against early repayment of debt, but it does not protect against extension risk. What type of tranche is it?
    A) planned amortization class
    B) support class
    C) companion class
    D) targeted amortization class

65. A broker completes a purchase of a callable corporate bond on behalf of a customer. Which of the following is NOT required to be included on the transaction confirmation to the buyer?
    A) disclosure of the call provision
    B) purchase price
    C) transaction date
    D) whether the seller was short or long

66. ABC stock closes at a spot price of $445 on Jun expiry. Which of the following long butterflies is worth the MOST at that time?
    A) ABC Jun 450/470/490 call butterfly
    B) ABC Jun 400/445/490 call butterfly
    C) ABC Jul 400/445/490 call butterfly
    D) ABC Sep 400/445/490 call butterfly

67. Which of the following is essential to "knowing the customer," according to FINRA?
    A) reviewing accounts of the customer at other institutions
    B) recognizing the customer's appearance
    C) understanding the authority of each person acting on behalf of the customer
    D) meeting periodically with the customer or those acting on the customer's behalf

68. A customer with $2,000 of account equity buys $4,000 worth of RSTU stock in a Regulation T margin account with no other positions. If the value of RSTU stock drops by 45%, taking the position value down to $2,600, at LEAST how much cash must the customer deposit to meet Regulation T minimum margin requirements?

   A) $0
   B) $50
   C) $650
   D) $1,400

69. An options trader with a somewhat bullish outlook is confident that GH stock will not fall when quarterly earnings are reported in early September. He believes the stock price will almost certainly remain stable near its current price of $30.00 or perhaps rise slightly. Which of the following trades BEST expresses his view?

   A) sell GH Sep 30 put at $1.50
   B) buy GH Sep 30 put for $1.50
   C) sell GH Sep 30 call at $1.50
   D) buy GH Sep 30 call for $1.50

70. What is the P/E ratio of a company that averages quarterly earnings per share of $3.00 with a stock price of $240?

   A) 80
   B) 60
   C) 40
   D) 20

71. Which of the following options strategies can be established by buying an out-of-the-money put option while also selling an out-of-the-money call option for the same underlier?

   A) straddle
   B) strangle
   C) risk reversal
   D) reverse conversion

72. Which of the following nationally recognized statistical rating organizations is NOT considered to be one of the "Big Three"?

   A) S&P Global Ratings
   B) Egan-Jones Ratings Company
   C) Moody's Investors Service
   D) Fitch Ratings

73. How does the inclusion of a call provision affect the price of a municipal bond when compared to a bond with the same terms and characteristics but no call provision?

   A) A bond with a call provision costs less than a bond without a call provision.
   B) A bond with a call provision costs more than a bond without a call provision.
   C) A bond with a call provision costs the same as a bond without a call provision.
   D) Not enough information is given to determine the effect of the call provision.

74. A member holds an open order from a customer to buy 3,000 shares of WX stock for $53.22 or better. The limit order is marked only as "good-'til-canceled," and WX stock pays a quarterly cash dividend of $1.02. What price should the limit be modified to on the next ex-dividend date, 1 week from today?

   A) $54.24
   B) $53.22 (no change)
   C) $52.20
   D) $49.14

75. A member sells broker-dealer services on the premises of a retail financial institution via a networking arrangement. Which of the following disclosures is the member required to make to customers opening an account there?

   A) Stocks are insured by the FDIC, but bonds are not.
   B) Bonds are insured by the FDIC, but options are not.
   C) Options are insured by the FDIC, but stocks are not.
   D) Securities products are not insured by the FDIC.

76. Which of the following describes a margin account where the customer's required equity is calculated based on risk exposure of the account's holdings rather than on their nominal value?

   A) Regulation T
   B) portfolio margin
   C) escrow margin
   D) receive versus payment

77. A customer believes that the stock of XYZ Corp. is vastly undervalued, so she liquidates all of her positions and uses some of the proceeds to buy 10 XYZ Jan 12 call contracts. On Jan expiry, she exercises those listed contracts because they are exactly $2.50 in-the-money at the closing bell. What does the customer receive upon settlement of this exercise?

    A) $2,500 cash
    B) $25,000 cash
    C) 1,000 long shares of XYZ stock
    D) 1,000 short shares of XYZ stock

78. Which of the following is considered an industrial development revenue bond?

    A) Biggs City issues debt to construct a warehouse, leases the warehouse to a private freight transport company, and uses the lease payments to fund the debt service.
    B) Robbinsville builds a six-lane toll road and uses toll revenue to fund the debt service.
    C) Thomas Heights issues debt, backed by the full faith and credit of the city, to build an industrial plant for a group of companies with plans to use tax revenue from the plant to fund the debt service.
    D) Warrenton issues debt to drill six new water wells in an area of town where many laborers live.

79. Bond H pays a coupon of 11% and is rated BBB by S&P Global Ratings. Bond K pays a coupon of 2% and is rated B by S&P Global Ratings. Based on this information, which of the bonds is usually described as "investment grade"?

    A) bond H
    B) bond K
    C) bonds H and K
    D) neither bond

80. Which of the following terms is intended to describe a business's annual net income divided by its shareholder equity? (Define "shareholder equity" as assets minus liabilities.)

    A) acid-test ratio
    B) net profit ratio
    C) return on equity
    D) quick assets

81. A customer sells 10,000 shares of EF stock at an average price of $29.45, versus a cost basis of $32.14, to close out a long position. Which of the following transactions, if subsequently made, would result in a wash sale?

    A) short sale of 10,000 shares of EF stock, 7 days later
    B) purchase of 100 contracts of EF Dec 25 put, 10 days later
    C) purchase of 100 contracts of EF Dec 25 call, 20 days later
    D) purchase of 10,000 shares of EF stock, 40 days later

82. Which of the following options trades would establish an iron condor?

    A) buy 1 XYZ Sep 20 call, sell 2 XYZ Sep 25 calls, buy 1 XYZ Sep 30 call
    B) sell 1 XYZ Sep 15 put, buy 1 XYZ Sep 20 put, buy 1 XYZ Sep 25 call, sell 1 XYZ Sep 30 call
    C) buy 1 XYZ Sep 15 put, sell 1 XYZ Sep 20 put, sell 1 XYZ Sep 20 call, buy 1 XYZ Sep 25 call
    D) buy 1 XYZ Sep 15 put, sell 1 XYZ Sep 20 put, sell 1 XYZ Sep 25 put, buy 1 XYZ Sep 30 put

83. Investment bank Gregory and Sons sells 10,000 XYZ Nov 40 put contracts to Smart Fir Investments on a day when the open interest for that contract is 4,322. Neither Gregory and Sons nor Smart Fir Investments has an existing position in the XYZ Nov 40 puts. Apart from this transaction, no XYZ Nov 40 puts trade on the day. What is the open interest for the subsequent trading day?

    A) 4,322
    B) 10,000
    C) 14,322
    D) 24,322

84. An option seller is short one contract of the NOPQ Jun 30 put, which he sold at $4.00 on a commission-free basis when NOPQ stock was trading at $29.20. The put option is assigned upon expiry, and the option seller is left with a long position of 100 shares of NOPQ stock. What is his cost basis?

    A) $25.20
    B) $26.00
    C) $33.20
    D) $34.00

85. Which of the following is NOT defined by the SEC as "investment discretion"?
    A) having the authorization to determine what securities to buy or sell in an account
    B) making transaction decisions even though someone else is responsible for those decisions
    C) convincing those with trading authorization to make transaction decisions in a certain way
    D) exercising influence over transactions in a way that SEC rules define as investment discretion

86. How often are short-interest figures for individual US-listed stocks updated?
    A) once a month
    B) twice a month
    C) once a week
    D) twice a week

87. How long does it take for a "regular way" listed option exercise to settle, if the underlier of the option is an exchange-traded fund such as SPY?
    A) T + 0
    B) T + 1
    C) T + 2
    D) T + 3

88. Today is June 20. Which of these long option strategies, all expiring this year, is most valuable?
    A) QRS Aug 30-strike straddle
    B) QRS Sep 30-strike straddle
    C) QRS Oct 30-strike put
    D) QRS Oct 30-strike straddle

89. According to SEC Regulation S-P, at LEAST how often must existing customers be provided with a clear, conspicuous notice that accurately reflects privacy policies and practices?
    A) annually
    B) semiannually
    C) once every 2 years
    D) upon every change to privacy policies and practices

90. In what currency is a eurodollar bond denominated if it is held in Japan and issued by an entity incorporated in the United Kingdom?
    A) euros
    B) dollars
    C) yen
    D) pounds sterling

91. What is the breakeven for a long QRS Jan 30/50 call spread? The best bid for the QRS Jan 30 call is $12.20, and it is offered at $12.60. The bid for the QRS Jan 50 call is $3.40, and it is offered at $4.00.
    A) $38.20
    B) $38.60
    C) $38.80
    D) $39.20

92. Which of the following measures of yield is MOST likely greatest for a noncallable "rising star" debt security that was rated Caa2 by Moody's shortly after its issuance at par but is now rated A3?
    A) nominal yield
    B) current yield
    C) yield to maturity
    D) yield to call

93. An options trader pays $30.45 to purchase a TUV Oct 400 straddle and also sells a TUV Oct 420/440 call spread at a credit of $12.25. What is her profit if TUV closes at $429.77 on Oct expiry?
    A) $2,000
    B) $1,820
    C) $200
    D) $180

94. A brokerage account is held by three friends, Ahmad, Brianna, and Charlie, as tenants in common. Ahmad owns a 50% interest, Brianna owns 25%, and Charlie owns 25%. If Charlie passes away, to whom does Charlie's quarter of the account go?
    A) Ahmad
    B) Brianna
    C) the person indicated in Charlie's will
    D) Half to Ahmad and half to Brianna

95. Which of these strategies has the greatest intrinsic value when RST stock is trading at $77.00?
    A) RST Jan 80 put, offered at $4.15
    B) RST Feb 65/70 call spread, offered at $4.70
    C) RST Mar 78 straddle, offered at $12.10
    D) RST Apr 70/75/80 put butterfly, offered at $2.55

96. According to the Securities Exchange Act of 1934, when a callable debt security with a maturity date that is subject to change trades on a current yield basis, the transaction confirmation must include all of the following EXCEPT
    A) call legend.
    B) yield to maturity.
    C) current yield.
    D) dollar price.

97. The spot price of EFGH stock is $860. Which of the following options is in-the-money?
    A) EFGH Jan 800 put
    B) EFGH Aug 800 call
    C) EFGH Dec 860 call
    D) EFGH Oct 900 call

98. Offerings exempted under Tier 2 of Regulation A are limited to $75 million or less in a 12-month period. What is the limitation for offerings exempted under Tier 1 of Regulation A in a 12-month period?
    A) $10 million
    B) $20 million
    C) $25 million
    D) $50 million

99. What is the point of maximum payout upon Mar expiry for a portfolio consisting of 1 short ABC Mar 45/50/55 put butterfly, 1 long ABC Mar 60/70/80 call butterfly, and 1 long ABC Mar 50/70/90 call butterfly? ABC stock is presently trading at $57.20.
    A) $50.00
    B) $60.00
    C) $70.00
    D) $80.00

100. For an ordinary offering of a security with average daily trading volume over $100,000, by an issuer with a common stock public float of at least $25 million, when does the restricted period under Regulation M begin?
    A) 1 business day before the pricing of the offering
    B) 2 business days before the pricing of the offering
    C) 5 business days before the pricing of the offering
    D) 10 business days before the pricing of the offering

101. Which of the following investment strategies is MOST exposed to systematic risk?
    A) merger arbitrage
    B) long-only equity
    C) market-neutral quantitative
    D) capital-structure arbitrage

102. An options market maker sells 5,000 QRS Jun 35 put contracts at $2.55 and hedges the risk by selling 250,000 shares of QRS stock at $35.20. He holds this position and does not actively adjust the stock hedge. Two months later, the QRS Jun 35 put has $0.30 of time value, and QRS stock is trading at $28.70. What is the market maker's loss on this QRS position as hedged? (Ignore the cost of borrowing the short shares.)
    A) $200,000
    B) $400,000
    C) $1,625,000
    D) $2,025,000

103. An investor owns 70,000 shares of STU stock. She intends to spend $80,000 on protective Mar put options. The investor can buy the Mar 50 put for $8.00, the Mar 45 put for $4.00, or the Mar 40 put for $2.00, and she would spend $80,000 in premium regardless of which put option she selects. Of these three different contracts, which put would provide the MOST protection if STU stock closes at $30.00 upon Mar options expiry?
    A) STU Mar 50 put
    B) STU Mar 45 put
    C) STU Mar 40 put
    D) A and C equally

104. Whose authorization is required for a customer to transfer shares of XYZ stock from her securities account at Brokerage A to her securities account at Brokerage B?

- A) the customer
- B) the customer and Brokerage A
- C) the customer and Brokerage B
- D) the customer, Brokerage A, and Brokerage B

105. Robert and Susan have a joint tenancy account with rights of survivorship. Robert designates Thomas as his sole beneficiary in his will. To whom does Robert's stake in the account go if Robert passes away?

- A) Susan only
- B) Thomas only
- C) Robert's estate
- D) Half to Susan and half to Thomas

106. Tiana owns 15 ABC Apr 88 put contracts and 798 shares of ABC stock in a cash account. The price of ABC falls to $49 in early April, and she decides to exercise as many put contracts as possible. At most, how many of the 15 ABC Apr 88 put contracts is she able to exercise?

- A) zero contracts
- B) seven contracts
- C) eight contracts
- D) fifteen contracts

107. BCD stock is trading at $71. In terms of premium, which of the following long option strategies (expiring this year) costs the most?

- A) BCD Apr 70/80 strangle
- B) BCD Apr 70 straddle
- C) BCD May 70/80 strangle
- D) BCD May 70 straddle

108. Under what circumstances would an equity trade consummated on or within the NBBO be considered a trade-through?

- A) if the trade price equals the bid price
- B) if the trade price equals the offer price
- C) if the trade price equals the last price
- D) under no circumstances

109. Section 28(e) of the Securities Exchange Act of 1934 establishes a safe harbor for arrangements where more than the lowest available commission is paid, provided the money manager

- A) believes that the commission is fair in relation to brokerage and research services provided.
- B) attempts in good faith to minimize transactions that overpay commissions.
- C) is unaware that a substantially better commission is available in the marketplace.
- D) is not directly or indirectly employed by the brokerage to whom commissions are paid.

110. Which of the following describes a quotation that can immediately be traded?

- A) nominal quote
- B) subject quote
- C) firm quote
- D) indicative quote

111. Jonathan has a traditional IRA. He was born on February 2, 1952. By what date must he begin taking required minimum distributions?

- A) April 1, 2023
- B) April 1, 2024
- C) April 1, 2025
- D) April 1, 2026

112. Account 12345, held with Broker Q, is designated as an error account. However, the account holder wants to begin using Account 12345 to buy call options on the equity of semiconductor equipment manufacturers. Whose approval is required to designate Account 12345 as something other than an error account?

- A) No approval is required.
- B) Approval of the account holder is required.
- C) Approval of the registered representative is required.
- D) Approval of the registered principal is required.

113. An electronics retailer with an average inventory of $40 million had sales revenue of $320 million in the preceding fiscal year, with a gross profit margin of 50%. What was her inventory turnover ratio for the preceding fiscal year?
    A) 0.5
    B) 2
    C) 4
    D) 8

114. Which of the following acts of Congress requires that debt issues regulated under the Securities Act of 1933 and exceeding a certain size of issuance be formalized with a document wherein terms and provisions are clearly enumerated?
    A) Securities Exchange Act of 1934
    B) Trust Indenture Act of 1939
    C) Investment Company Act of 1940
    D) Investment Advisers Act of 1940

115. How are investment-grade bonds typically quoted in the OTC US credit market?
    A) dollar price
    B) yield to maturity
    C) yield spread to benchmark
    D) current yield

116. Edwin shorted 600 shares of DEF stock at $22.10 and sold six contracts of the DEF Jun 22 put at $4.10. He holds no other securities. If DEF stock closes at $6.77 on Jun expiry and all of Edwin's put contracts are assigned, what is Edwin's profit?
    A) $2,460
    B) $2,520
    C) $9,198
    D) $11,658

117. Which of the following put spreads is worth the HIGHEST premium?
    A) HIJK Dec 30/15 put spread
    B) HIJK Dec 30/20 put spread
    C) HIJK Dec 30/25 put spread
    D) HIJK Dec 25/10 put spread

118. Which of the following is generally NOT a difference between SPX options and SPY options?
    A) SPX options are cash settled, whereas SPY options are physically settled.
    B) SPX options are European style, whereas SPY options are American style.
    C) SPX options have no one underlying instrument, whereas SPY options have SPY as the underlier.
    D) SPX options trade only during market hours, whereas SPY options trade around the clock.

119. Which of the following types of preferred stock gets a share of the common stockholders' payout in case of liquidation?
    A) cumulative
    B) noncumulative
    C) participating
    D) nonparticipating

120. Barbara bought a protective put spread to hedge her long UVW shares. She owns 100 shares of UVW stock that were purchased for an average price of $106. She is long 1 UVW Dec 100 put that she bought for $5.00, and she is short 1 UVW Dec 90 put that she sold at $2.00. What is Barbara's overall realized loss on this UVW position if she sells all of her UVW shares at $80.00 in the closing auction on Dec expiry?
    A) $2,600 loss
    B) $1,900 loss
    C) $700 loss
    D) $300 loss

121. Xavier is confident that JKL stock will rally far beyond its present price of $52, so he buys 1 JKL Sep 60 call for $3, sells 1 JKL Sep 50 put at $5, and buys 1 JKL Dec 80 call for $12. What is Xavier's profit (or loss) on Sep expiry if JKL stock closes at $59? (Assume that the Dec 80 call has $11 of time value.)
    A) $100 loss
    B) $100 gain
    C) $200 loss
    D) $300 gain

122. Treasury stock is held by whom?
   A) the US Treasury
   B) the issuer of the stock
   C) shareholders of the company
   D) nobody

123. Which of these bonds is MOST likely to be redeemed early by its issuer when 10-year rates fall?
   A) 10-year debenture with call provision and no make-whole provision
   B) 10-year bullet bond
   C) 10-year debenture with put provision
   D) 10-year debenture with make-whole call provision

124. Juana shorted $600,000 worth of stocks across a broad range of sectors, and she bought a single SPX Index 3500 call contract to hedge the short exposure. At expiry, the SPX Index 3500 call is exercised in-the-money. The stocks in Juana's short position have rallied by 5% on average since the position was opened. What is Juana's short position now?
   A) short $600,000 worth of stocks
   B) short $630,000 worth of stocks
   C) short $250,000 worth of stocks
   D) short $280,000 worth of stocks

125. Lightning Brokers uses advertising to encourage retail investors to "open an account today and day-trade like the professionals!" Under what condition can Lightning Brokers open an account for a customer who has not received a Day-Trading Risk Disclosure Statement?
   A) The customer has attested in writing that he will not use the account for day-trading purposes.
   B) Lightning Brokers approves the customer for day-trading in accordance with FINRA criteria.
   C) Lightning Brokers prepares a record setting forth the basis upon which the account is approved.
   D) This is never permissible.

126. Which of the following is NOT considered to be a fiduciary duty?
   A) duty to seek best execution
   B) duty to fully and fairly disclose all conflicts of interest
   C) duty of profitability
   D) duty of informed consent

127. Rodney sells a CDEF Aug 45/65 strangle at $8. At which of the following prices of CDEF stock would this strangle result in a loss for Rodney upon Aug expiry?
   A) $35
   B) $45
   C) $60
   D) $70

128. In 12 months, ABC stock has increased from $34 to today's closing price of $90. ABC's 12-month moving average is $39, its 9-month moving average is $61, its 6-month moving average is $86, and its 3-month moving average is $88. ABC options volatility is near an all-time low. Which of the following terms describes ABC stock's price action in the past 3 months?
   A) breakout
   B) consolidation
   C) support
   D) oversold

129. FGH Widgets Incorporated reduces its cost of goods sold without changing the price that its customers pay per widget, without affecting the number of widgets sold, and without affecting the company's fixed costs. What effect does this have on the company's operating income?
   A) Operating income increases.
   B) Operating income does not change.
   C) Operating income decreases.
   D) Not enough information is provided.

130. When must a credit trader locate borrow for the short sale of a corporate bond?
   A) before the trade
   B) before the settlement date
   C) within 2 business days of settlement
   D) Locates are not required in an over-the-counter transaction.

131. Why was the ACATS system created?
    A) to display and report over-the-counter fixed-income securities transactions
    B) to provide real-time reporting of equity transactions matched on alternative trading systems
    C) to move customer accounts between firms
    D) to clear and settle equity securities transactions

132. What is the time value of a DEF Nov 65 straddle that is worth a premium of $18 if DEF stock is currently trading at $61?
    A) $4
    B) $8
    C) $14
    D) $18

133. During market hours, when the last trade price ("reference price") of an exchange-listed security was over $25.00 but not higher than $50.00, FINRA uses a 5% threshold to determine whether the subsequent transaction is clearly erroneous. As a percentage of its last trade price of $32.40, what is the clearly erroneous transaction threshold for a single stock outside of market hours?
    A) 3%
    B) 5%
    C) 6%
    D) 10%

134. XYZ Corp. holds a shareholder vote to fill three board seats from a pool of seven candidates, using cumulative voting. Sonia owns 700 XYZ shares, with one vote per share. How many votes can she cast for her favorite candidate?
    A) 100
    B) 700
    C) 2,100
    D) 4,900

135. Which of the following terms describes an over-allotment option granted to the underwriter of an initial public offering if demand for the issue exceeds expectations?
    A) call
    B) convertible
    C) greenshoe
    D) concession

Answer Key

1. **B)** FINRA prohibits correspondence or retail communication that cherry-picks specific past recommendations that would have generated a profit. However, lists of all recommendations by a member firm for "the same type, kind, grade or classification of securities" from the past year or longer are permitted. In this case, the associated person may indeed list this profitable recommendation by itself. The statement must include, "it should not be assumed that recommendations made in the future will be profitable or will equal the performance of the securities in this list." The associated person must also include the security name, recommended action, date and price at that time, recommended target entry price, and current price.

2. **A)** Common stock is junior to debt in the capital structure of a company. If the company cannot cover its debt burden, then there will be no money left over for distribution to shareholders. The equity value is thus $0. The loss incurred by the trader per underlying share is equal to $45.00 (in other words, the maximum intrinsic value of a 45-strike put) minus the premium of $3.50 collected when the put was sold. This difference is $41.50 which, when computed using the 100 contract multiplier, comes to a net loss of $4,150 per contract. Since the trader sold three contracts, his net loss was three times this amount: $12,450.

3. **C)** Collateralized mortgage obligations (CMOs) are a complicated product with esoteric correlation risks. These risks are generally considered to have been a contributing factor to the Great Recession. Before selling CMOs to any person except an institutional investor, FINRA requires that a member firm provide educational materials about CMO structure, characteristics, risks, terminology, and key facts.

4. **A)** Dark pools are an increasingly active venue for equity transactions, and nearly every major bank operates one. Dark pool transactions must be reported to a FINRA Trade Reporting Facility (TRF) within 10 seconds of execution.

5. **D)** According to FINRA Rule 2165, members have a safe harbor to pause disbursements and account transfers for customers 65 or older. This intervention must be based on a reasonable belief that exploitation has taken place, will take place, or is taking place, and it must be immediately investigated. Notification must be given within 2 business days, and the hold cannot persist beyond 15 business days unless the member's initial belief about the occurrence of exploitation is justified by investigation.

6. **B)** Backing away is the practice of providing ostensibly firm quotations but then qualifying them or refusing to trade when the customer responds with an interest to trade at that level. This is a prohibited practice. Option A describes spoofing; Option C describes "painting the tape"; Option D describes front-running. These three practices are considered manipulative and/or exploitative and are also prohibited.

7. **C)** A broker-dealer should not make recommendations that are unsuitable for a customer who receives them. If a broker-dealer does the work to specifically tailor smart and suitable recommendations for its customers, there is no problem with a customer benefiting from this effort and transacting every such recommendation. However, FINRA views suitability as a three-part question: 1) there must be a reasonable basis for the recommendation; 2) the recommendation must fit the customer's specific investment profile, risk tolerance, and objectives; 3) the recommendation must be quantitatively contextualized within the broader

picture of the customer's existing positions, transaction costs, and other recommendations being made by the broker-dealer. Option C correctly touches on this third point of quantitative suitability because while each recommendation may be good, taking them all together would expose the investor to excessive risk.

8. **B)** Taping firms are member firms with a prevalent number of registered persons who are linked, either directly or by working at a disciplined member firm, with disciplinary history from the past 3 years. FINRA requires these firms to tape-record the telemarketing activities of their registered persons. For a firm that employs more than 20,000 persons, the taping threshold is crossed when 20% or more of the registered persons are associated with disciplinary history. A member that is designated as a taping firm for the first time can reduce its staffing levels in order to fall below the taping threshold, but it must identify the terminated persons to FINRA and may not rehire any of those people for 180 days.

9. **A)** To answer this question, use the process of elimination, starting from the bottom. Selling a call spread, as in Option D, would mean that the customer makes more money when the stock declines than when it appreciates; this doesn't fit a bullish customer. Buying a put spread (Option C) would express a bearish viewpoint, which also doesn't fit the customer. Buying an at-the-money long call (Option B) would certainly express a bullish viewpoint, but the call would lose value if the implied volatility of options declines. This leaves the short put in Option A, which expresses a bullish viewpoint but also allows the customer to profit if option prices decay due to a reduced expectation of future volatility. Here, the customer seeks long delta and short kappa. This means that she must sell options, and the resulting position must have a net-positive directional exposure to the underlier.

10. **A)** The limit order was transacted correctly; the only mistake here was the execution report. While this miscommunication may have resulted in hedge losses or a missed profit opportunity, the customer must know the trade as actually executed and confirmed in the corrected report. Some frustration is certainly justified, and the customer may react with specific demands or even file a formal complaint. Even so, there is no basis for the exchange to cancel the trade or for the floor broker to assume any profit or loss for the customer. Using an error account to do so would violate NYSE rules.

11. **B)** Each member is responsible for investigating the good character, business reputation, qualifications, and experience of the employees that it sponsors for FINRA registration. Part of this process includes a review of the most recent Form U5 for an employee, which corresponds to the termination of the employee's status as an associated person of a previous employer. However, if this is not possible, the member shall demonstrate to FINRA that it has made a reasonable effort to review the most recent Form U5.

12. **A)** The maximum possible value of a butterfly is determined by its strike width. All of the butterflies presented in the question have a maximum payout of $10. Assuming that DEF closes at $30 upon expiry, the butterfly in Options A and C would be worth $10; the butterfly in Option B would be worthless; and the butterfly in Option D would be worth $5. The most sensible position for a customer who believes that DEF will close at $30 upon expiration in 6 months is the long butterfly centered at $30. There will be a difference in price between different butterflies of the same width and maturity, but this strategy does not carry outsized directional risk. The major question is mainly where the stock will trade at expiry.

13. **C)** Cold calls—calls that are not predicated on an existing business or personal relationship—are not permitted before 8:00 a.m. or after 9:00 p.m. in the called party's location.

14. **A)** By selling the 40 call, the customer collects a premium of $2.40 per share. This option premium gives her a cushion, insofar as ABC stock can decline by that amount without incurring a loss. She bought shares for $38.00, so if ABC stock declines by the amount of the premium, the price of ABC becomes $35.60 and the customer breaks even. The trade-off is that her maximum possible gains are capped at

$4.40 per share because they are short the 40 call. They would keep the option premium and make money as the stock rallies to $40.00, but any gains in the stock beyond the $40.00 mark would cancel out with losses on the option.

15. **C)** One of the tax advantages of inherited stock that has appreciated since the time of acquisition is a stepped-up cost basis. The cost basis was $2 originally, but the cost basis of inherited stock resets based on its value on the date of the decedent's death. In this case, the stepped-up cost basis is $100. The grandson does not owe tax on the inherited stock, and he would be subject to long-term capital gains tax versus the stepped-up basis if he sells the stock.

16. **B)** Income from dividends is the most attractive characteristic of YZ stock, based on the information given. A stock that pays high dividends is generally not a growth stock because growth companies tend to reinvest profits into their business rather than distributing those profits as dividends. There is no apparent reason why buying and holding YZ stock would be an arbitrage of any sort. While the investor says the price of YZ stick may be speculative, she says she was attracted to this investment due to its stable share price and did not mention any upcoming catalysts or reasons for an upside breakout. By all appearances, she simply wants to hold YZ and collect dividend income.

17. **A)** The cost basis for an assigned put is the strike price minus the net premium initially collected ($200 − $15 = $185).

18. **C)** The yield to call would be the lowest for a bond that is trading at a premium. A bond with a nominal yield of 10% and 8% yield to maturity would be trading at a premium because the yield is less than the stated or coupon rate. Options A, B, and D are discount bonds, so they would likely show yield to maturity.

19. **C)** Municipal securities advertisement, in accordance with Municipal Securities Rulemaking Board (MSRB) Rule G-21(f), is approved by the firm's securities principal (municipal or general) and maintained by the firm. The NYSE, the SEC, and the MSRB do not approve municipal securities advertisement.

20. **A)** Treasury notes pay coupons, so their nominal yield should never be zero. Long-term interest rates in the United States are positive as a matter of policy, so the current yield of a Treasury note should also never be zero. When a bond trades near par, that means the coupon ("nominal") yield roughly equals the market-determined ("current") yield. This can happen with off-the-run Treasurys (not the most recently auctioned ones) if the market-determined yield hovers near the coupon yield.

21. **B)** The Direct Registration System (DRS) allows assets to be moved electronically and with little effort. This enables a very large volume of stock to change hands without extraordinarily long settlement times. Some shareholders prefer to bear physical stock certificates. Others hold shares in street name, simplifying their interactions with their brokerage firms and allowing their brokers to clear only their net transacted share differences through the National Securities Clearing Corporation (NSCC). Treasury stock is not held in any investor's name; it is stock that was previously outstanding, later reacquired by the issuer.

22. **D)** Not every quotation is firm. When communicating quotations to customers, registered representatives are expected to honor firm quotations. It is good practice to explicitly state when a quotation is subject or given for indicative purposes only. Refusal to honor a firm quotation is considered by FINRA to be "backing away," but a broker-dealer is not obligated to transact subject quotations.

23. **C)** The investor earns a profit of $2,600 on the option contract because it cost him $4 to cover the put and a premium of $30 was initially collected ($30 − $4 = $26; using the 100 multiplier, $26 × 100 = $2,600). Profits from short options are not eligible for long-term capital gains regardless of the holding period; they are taxed as short-term capital gains.

24. **D)** Even though the HIJKL share class is qualitatively superior to the HIJK share class, the free market will decide the relative valuation of the two classes of shares. It might seem that nonvoting HIJK shares should be cheaper than the voting HIJKL shares because they do not empower the shareholder as much. Consider,

however, a scenario in which HIJK Robotics Corporation carries out a buyback only on HIJK shares: excess demand for HIJK will lift its price without directly affecting the price of HIJKL. Consider a similar scenario in which an activist investor liquidates holdings in HIJKL: excess supply of HIJKL will suppress its price without directly affecting the price of HIJK. Based on the information in the question, it is unclear which share class should trade over the other.

25. **B)** A customer with a margin account can post equity and borrow funds from the broker to buy and sell securities. If the value of these securities declines beyond a certain threshold, the customer will typically be asked to post additional equity (a "margin call"). Depending on market conditions, the broker sometimes liquidates holdings of an account immediately without contacting the customer first. Liquidation based solely on a decline in market value does not happen in a cash account, which is fully capitalized by the customer. Some IRAs allow what is known as "limited margin." Limited margin in a retirement account typically permits a customer to borrow against impending settlements, but it is not a means for the customer to use additional leverage.

26. **C)** In addition to the potential for deferred sales loads and other fees, variable annuities that are withdrawn early can be subject to tax penalties. Marketing materials may not misrepresent variable annuities as a short-term or liquid investment, and any discussion of the ease of withdrawing funds from a variable annuity must be accompanied by clear language describing the costs of early redemption.

27. **B)** Options on SPY, like other listed equity options, settle T + 1. A transaction effected on Tuesday will settle on the next business day: Wednesday.

28. **D)** The price-to-earnings (P/E) ratio of a company is defined as the share price of the stock divided by the company's 12-month earnings per share. The P/E ratio is sometimes calculated based on the trailing four quarters, which makes sense when a company is involved in a cyclical business (for example, toy sales or greeting cards). This is called a trailing P/E ratio. In other circumstances, such as for a company in a rapidly expanding business, the P/E ratio may be calculated based on guidance about future earnings. This is called a forward P/E ratio. Using the information provided in the question: an earnings per share of $12 for the recent fiscal year and a share price of $600, the ratio of share price to earnings can be computed as 50 ($600 ÷ $12 = $50).

29. **B)** FINRA Rule 11892 establishes criteria for whether a transaction in a single exchange-listed security is clearly erroneous. A FINRA officer will compare the execution price to that of the last trade immediately before it (the reference price). If a discrepancy between an execution and its reference price is greater than a certain threshold percentage of the reference price, the transaction is clearly erroneous. For transactions during normal market hours, the threshold percentage is defined as 10% if the reference price is $25 or less; 5% if the reference price is greater than $25 but no greater than $50; and 3% if the reference price is greater than $50. Qualitatively, this means that bigger relative jumps in price are permitted for cheaper stocks.

FINRA notes that the reference price may be different in cases of "relevant news impacting a security." This would likely apply when a stock is halted for impending bad news, eliminating Options A and C. In Option D, the reference price is $21.00, and the threshold percentage for that reference price is 10%, so a discontinuity of $2.00 would not be clearly erroneous because it is less than $2.10. Option B describes a reference price of $26.00, and the threshold percentage for that reference price is 5%, so a discontinuity of $2.00 would be clearly erroneous because it is greater than $1.30.

30. **A)** For the purpose of marking order tickets, each independent trading unit (colloquially called a "desk") at the trader's firm is permitted to aggregate its share position irrespective of the firm's overall position in that security. The trader should mark her ticket as a long sale because her account, and thus her aggregation unit, holds a long position in excess of the 10,000 shares of PQR stock that she will sell today. There is no such thing as a "long-exempt sale" in Regulation SHO.

31. **C)** A long straddle consists of a long put and a long call with identical strike and maturity;

a short straddle consists of a short put and a short call with identical strike and maturity. If one contract in a straddle is a long XYZ Jan 20 put, then the other contract is necessarily a long XYZ Jan 20 call (Option C).

32. **D)** A European-style option allows the long holder to make an exercise decision only at maturity. American-style options are slightly more permissive. An American-style option allows the long holder to make an exercise decision either at maturity or, irreversibly, on any business day before maturity. An American-style option that expires in September can be exercised in September and August, but it cannot be exercised in October after it has expired.

33. **B)** In the United States, a debenture is an unsecured bond that is not collateralized by a claim on specific assets or cash flows thereof. When issued by a corporation, a debenture falls in the more junior portion of the capital structure. Typically, in the event of bankruptcy, holders of a debenture may recover some of their investment after holders of more senior collateralized debt are made whole. An equipment trust certificate (ETC) is a form of debt that is commonly used to purchase commercial aircraft. Residential mortgage-backed securities (RMBSs) are collateralized with homes, and the cash flows of credit card asset–backed securities (ABS) are derived from a pool of credit card debt.

34. **C)** The Bond Buyer Index, also known as the BB40 Index, has been published daily since 1985. It is based on the prices of 40 actively traded, recently issued, long-term municipal bonds.

35. **A)** A high-yield bond with a 2% nominal yield is likely to trade at a substantial discount in comparison to the other securities mentioned. The price of high-yield bonds (sometimes known as junk bonds) is determined by a combination of three factors: 1) interest rates in general affect bond prices; 2) a company's likelihood of default affects bond prices because bonds get cheaper when they are less likely to be paid through to maturity; 3) a bond's recovery rate affects its price because a bond for which a smaller proportion of the initial investment can be recovered in bankruptcy is a far more painful investment in the case of a default. High-yield bonds are offered at a discount to Treasury and investment-grade debt because investors require a bargain-bin price to make up for the increased risk.

36. **C)** Think of the intrinsic value of an option as its in-the-money amount. The MNO Nov 18 put is in-the-money because the MNO market price of $16.25 is less than the put strike ($18.00). The difference between the put strike and the price of MNO amounts to an intrinsic value of $1.75 ($18.00 - $16.25 = $1.75).

37. **D)** In general, investors in mutual funds have the benefit of greater transparency and stronger federal and state legal protections than investors in hedge funds. Both investment vehicles have a fiduciary duty to investors, and both are prohibited from engaging in fraudulent behavior. Some small hedge funds are not required to file periodic reports with the SEC. For these reasons and others, Rule 506(b) imposes a maximum of thirty-five nonaccredited investors who may invest in a hedge fund offering.

38. **B)** Rule 12b-1 of the Investment Company Act of 1940 permits mutual funds to use fund assets for the purposes of marketing and distribution.

39. **D)** Mediation is a voluntary process for the resolution of grievances. It carries a high success rate and can be initiated at any time before or during a claim for arbitration. Mediation that is initiated during FINRA arbitration runs concurrently with the arbitration process, but the parties may jointly decide to suspend arbitration if they find a resolution through mediation. If the parties mediate through FINRA's mediation program, fees for adjournment of a concurrent arbitration case may be waived.

40. **C)** Expiring SPX options are settled with a cash payment based on the settlement value of the S&P 500 Index, which itself is based on the opening value of S&P 500 Index constituents in their respective primary markets. The investor collected a net credit of $60.00 at the time he sold this call calendar spread ($300.50 - $240.50 = $60.00). He was long an Apr call that expired worthless because it was out-of-the-money.

He was short a Jul call that expired with an exercise-settlement amount of $310.50 ($4,810.50 − $4,500 = $310.50). The exercise-settlement amount is equal to the intrinsic value of the Jul call upon expiration, and it is paid out to the long holder of the Jul call as cash on the business day after expiration. The investor's loss is the difference between the initial credit and the payout of the short call ($310.50 − $60.00 = $250.50). Using the 100 multiplier, he lost $25,050 ($250.50 × 100 = $25,050).

41. **A)** General obligation bonds are a common municipal debt instrument that is backed by the full faith and credit of the issuer. In contrast, a revenue bond is backed by cash flows from a specific project or activity, and a moral obligation bond is not technically backed by anything save for the issuer's desire to maintain its credit quality.

42. **A)** The speculator will pay long-term capital gains tax because his holding period exceeds 1 year. His cost basis is the purchase price of $40, and his sale price for the FGH 300 call is its intrinsic value of $90 versus a stock price of $390. Factoring in the 100 multiplier for this long-term equity anticipation security (LEAPS) option, that amounts to a profit of $5,000 ($90 − $40 = $50; $50 × 100 = $5,000).

43. **C)** An American depositary receipt (ADR) is US-issued stock in a foreign-listed company. This is accomplished when an affiliate of an American bank purchases shares of the company in the country where its equity is listed. The American bank issues stock that represents ownership of those shares held abroad. Only Option C describes such an arrangement. LMNO is not issued in the United States, so Option A can be eliminated. PQRS is not listed abroad, so Option B can be eliminated. Option D seems promising, but there are over 200 Chinese companies that—like XYZ—have chosen to tap in to US capital markets by offering equity directly in America.

44. **D)** The most susceptible security is the pass-through residential mortgage-backed security (RMBS) because it is characterized using assumptions about the debtor's prepayment behavior. If the debtor's real behavior is markedly different from those assumptions, duration extension can have a substantial impact on the cash flows provided and thus on the value of the debt. For example, a debtor is less likely to refinance (prepay) a mortgage if rates increase substantially. Duration is a characteristic of fixed-income products, so Option A can be excluded. Thirty-year Treasury bonds will mature in 30 years no matter what, so Option B can also be excluded. Corporate debentures may mature early due to call or put provisions, and their duration can change as a function of the convexity effects of such provisions; barring such provisions, the duration of a debenture is a fairly straightforward calculation.

45. **D)** The time value of an out-of-the-money put option is equal to its premium. Options that are out-of-the-money do not have intrinsic value.

46. **C)** If four bids are placed, and each bid is equal to a third of the size of the Treasury note offering, then the highest bidder will receive no allocation and the other three bidders will receive equal allocations at the second-highest yield bid. This Treasury note will be issued with a coupon rate of 1.64%.

47. **B)** Short-term gains can be misleading. As a result, FINRA rules prohibit investment company rankings based solely on total returns from a period of less than 1 year. Money market mutual funds, which invest in highly liquid short-term instruments, are excluded from this prohibition. Some of their holdings may include certificates of deposit, commercial paper, repurchase agreements, and Treasury bills. (Another exception to this rule is available if the rankings are based on yield rather than total returns.)

48. **C)** A breakpoint discount is a volume discount on the front-end sales load paid by a Class A mutual fund investor who invests more than a particular amount of money. When a mutual fund offers this volume discount, the breakpoint schedule will be described in the fund's prospectus and statement of additional information.

49. **D)** The Internal Revenue Code defines non-equity options as "section 1256 contracts." Section 1256 contracts also include foreign currency contracts and regulated futures

contracts. Forty percent of the gain or loss of a section 1256 contract is treated as short-term capital gain or loss, and the remaining 60% is treated as long-term capital gain or loss.

50. **B)** Regulation FD addresses selective disclosure of material nonpublic information by requiring that information shared with certain enumerated market participants also be fairly and fully disclosed to the public. This helps to level the playing field for market participants, including current shareholders as well as other investors whose future investment decisions in the issuer's securities may be affected by the information. One method of satisfying this requirement is to file a Form 8-K with the Securities and Exchange Commission.

51. **C)** The Internal Revenue Code establishes certain exclusions to the rules regarding taxable gifts. Known as "qualified transfers," these include medical costs and educational tuition, paid directly to the educational organization or medical care provider. Utility expenses would not qualify under either of these two exceptions to the gift tax, even if paid directly to the municipality providing the utilities. The exclusion for certain transfers for educational or medical expenses does not require a familial relationship between the giver and the recipient.

52. **A)** In an inflationary environment, prices rise over time. The cost of goods sold would be lower for earlier inventory than for later inventory, so the first-in-first-out (FIFO) accounting method would reflect a larger profit margin versus the same sales revenue. More profits result in a greater tax liability.

53. **D)** The customer bought 200 shares of CDEF for $20.20, sold 100 shares at $21.00 due to assignment in June, and sold 100 shares at $22.00 due to assignment in November. The profit from the shares is $80.00 plus $180 ($260 total). She collected a premium of $50.00 from the Jun 21 call and a premium of $25.00 from the Nov 22 call. The profit from the option premium is $75.00. The customer's profit from these CDEF trades is $260 from the shares and $75.00 from the option premium, for a total profit of $335.

54. **A)** The question asks which bond has the highest price. Among the answer options, two factors vary: maturity and yield. Traders in the US credit market often quote bonds in terms of a yield spread versus a benchmark security. This spread is typically communicated in terms of basis points. (Each basis point is 1.0% of 1.0%.) For example, a 30-year corporate bond might be benchmarked using the 30-year Treasury bond. A yield spread of +50 basis points, on top of a benchmark Treasury bond yield of 2.1%, results in a current yield of 2.6% for the corporate bond in Option A. Bond price and current yield have an inverse relationship. All else being equal, a bond with a lower yield costs more. Maturity and price have a direct relationship. A bond with more time to maturity costs more, all else being equal. The bond in Option A features the lowest yield (2.6%) as well as the longest maturity (30 years), so it will have the highest price.

55. **C)** Of the four transactions, only Option B (short calls) and Option C (long puts) would make money if EFG stock closes below $33.75 on expiry. The short calls in Option B would profit from the premium collected at the time of sale. The long puts in Option C would profit from an increase in intrinsic value. Below $33.50, Option C would be more profitable than Option B. If EFG stock falls to $32.00 and the time value of the options decays to zero (as is typical upon expiry), Option C would result in an options profit of $700,000 and Option B would result in an options profit of $100,000. Compare this to a loss of $800,000 on the investor's long EFG stock position. Option C would be the superior hedge in this scenario because the investor would lose only the premium paid for the long puts.

56. **A)** The trader has established an option structure with four contracts: 2 short XYZ Jun 35 calls, 1 long XYZ Jun 30 put, and 1 long XYZ Jun 30 call. The net premium for this option structure is a debit of $1.60, so any price of XYZ stock at which the option structure is intrinsically worth $1.60 would be considered a break-even level.

Option A is a break-even level; at a spot price of $28.40, the 3 calls have no intrinsic value and the Jun 30 put has an intrinsic value equal to the $1.60 premium paid for the option structure. Option B reflects a loss of the $1.60 premium paid; none of the four options have intrinsic value at a spot price of $30.00. Option C reflects a loss of $0.20; at $31.40, the put and the Jun 35 calls have no intrinsic value, but the Jun 30 call is intrinsically worth $1.40. Option D reflects a gain of $2.60; at $35.80, the put is worthless, but each short call has intrinsic value of $0.80, and the long call has intrinsic value of $5.80. Aside from Option A, other break-even levels for this structure are $31.60 and $38.40.

57. **C)** If OPQ stock goes to $0, each short Jan 30 put will have an intrinsic value of $30, representing a loss of $20 because the trader also collected a $10 premium when he wrote the puts. For three listed contracts with a 100 multiplier, that $20 per-share loss amounts to a net loss of $6,000 on the position.

58. **B)** Regulation S is a safe-harbor provision of the Securities Act of 1933 that was adopted in 1990. It establishes an exemption for SEC registration of securities that are neither sold nor offered to buyers in the United States. Option B accurately describes this market limitation of Regulation S securities.

59. **A)** The capital asset pricing model indicates that an asset with a beta of zero is expected to appreciate at the risk-free rate. When the risk-free rate increases, the asset's expected return increases too, as stated in Option A. The capital asset pricing model suggests that such an asset bears no risk premium even if the market as a whole is expected to rise at a rate that exceeds the risk-free rate.

60. **C)** The coupon cash flows of most municipal bonds in the United States have federal tax-exempt status. In addition, coupon income from a municipal bond is generally exempt from taxes paid to the state of issuance. So, an investor who receives interest income from a municipal bond issued within her state of residence likely pays lower tax at both the state and federal level than she would for a corporate bond with the same nominal yield. This is effectively a subsidy for the issuing state or municipality; investors generally accept lower yields when less coupon income is lost as tax, reducing the cost of funds for long-term municipal projects.

61. **B)** Listed equity option contracts are automatically adjusted for splits of the underlying security. Early exercise due to a split would throw away the option's time value without capturing any benefit in return. Options C and D can therefore be eliminated. Stock transactions on exchanges in the United States settle T + 2, so the ex-dividend date is 1 business day before the record date. Option A can be eliminated because a stock whose dividend has a record date of Tuesday will already be trading ex-dividend on Monday. The holder would be exercising 1 day too late to collect the dividend.

By process of elimination, the only remaining possibility is Option B. It would be profitable to exercise the call option on Monday and capture a $2.50 dividend with a record date of Wednesday. A $2.50 dividend for 100 shares (remember the contract multiplier) is worth $200 more than the contract's $50.00 time value. Call options are not automatically adjusted to account for regular dividends from the issuer of the underlying shares, but if the time value is less than the dividend amount, the holder of the option can exercise the option and relinquish its time value in order to capture the dividend.

62. **A)** Nonqualified dividends are typically taxed as ordinary income. They are also referred to as "ordinary" dividends.

63. **C)** FINRA Rule 409T establishes quarterly statement requirements for non-DVP/RVP accounts. An account with no holdings and/or transactions may have a cash balance, an interest credit, or some other activity. As in Option C, a brokerage may have no information to report for an account with no holdings, no cash, and no entries, in which case FINRA does not obligate the brokerage to provide a quarterly statement.

64. **D)** The terms support class and companion class mean the same thing, so Options B and C can be eliminated. Planned amortization class (PAC) tranches are senior to targeted amortization class (TAC) tranches because they protect against extension risk within a predetermined range of prepayment speed assumptions. TAC tranches amortize early repayment across the life of the security, but they may take longer than anticipated to repay because they offer no similar protection against late payment.

65. **D)** Purchase price and transaction date are required information for securities transaction

reports under Rule 10b-10 of the Securities Exchange Act of 1934, and the rule also requires disclosure of early redemption features of debt securities. This leaves Option D as the correct choice.

66. **B)** A long butterfly is an advanced options strategy that involves selling two contracts of the middle strike and buying one contract each of the outer strikes. The Jun 450/470/490 butterfly is worth nearly nothing at the close of trading on Jun expiry if ABC stock closes at $445, outside of the range of the outer strikes. No time value remains, and all of the intrinsic values of the four contracts in an out-of-the-money butterfly add up to zero (in this case, because each constituent call has an intrinsic value of zero). That leaves three possibilities that have differing times to maturity: zero months, 1 month, and 3 months. The maximum payoff for a long butterfly occurs upon the short strike at expiry. Since the spot price of $445 is equal to the middle (short) strike, the call butterfly with the least time to maturity—Option B—has the greatest value.

67. **C)** Members must use reasonable diligence to determine the essential facts about every customer as well as every person acting under the customer's authority. According to FINRA, the essential facts are "those required to (a) effectively service the customer's account; (b) act in accordance with any special handling instructions for the account; (c) understand the authority of each person acting on behalf of the customer; and (d) comply with applicable laws, regulations, and rules."

68. **B)** The customer's RSTU position is worth $2,600 after RSTU stock drops, and the Regulation T maintenance margin requirement is 25%, so her account equity must be $650 or greater. She lost $1,400 of her $2,000 when RSTU stock dropped, so she must deposit $50 to meet the maintenance margin requirement.

69. **A)** Options B and C can be eliminated because they express bearish views. The options trader does not expect a large move, so rather than paying a 5% premium for the GH Sep 30 call, he would be more likely to collect a 5% premium by selling the GH Sep 30 put, as in Option A.

70. **D)** Price-to-earnings (P/E) ratio is a comparison metric between share price and annual earnings. If the quarterly earnings per share (EPS) totals $3.00, then the annual EPS totals $12.00. The share price of $240 divided by this $12.00 figure amounts to a P/E ratio of 20.

71. **C)** A risk reversal, also known as a collar, can be used to bound a long or short stock position and limit losses in exchange for capping gains. Option C is correct; a risk reversal involves buying (or selling) a put while selling (or buying) a call at a higher strike price. For example, a trader who owns 100 shares of a stock can buy a downside put and sell an upside call to limit the position's profit-and-loss if the stock trades outside of the range of the strike prices. The sale of the short option helps to pay the premium of the long option.

72. **B)** Of the nine nationally recognized statistical rating organizations (NRSROs), the "Big Three" are S&P, Moody's, and Fitch. Egan-Jones stands among the remaining six.

73. **A)** Call provisions represent a right of the issuer. Their inclusion in a bond generally corresponds to an increase in yield to compensate for the additional risk of early redemption of the debt. All else being equal, a bond with a call provision costs less than a bond without such a feature.

74. **C)** Unless the order is marked "do not reduce," FINRA Rule 5330 stipulates that the member should subtract the cash dividend amount from the limit price of the order upon the ex-dividend date, before execution. In cases where this subtracted price is not quotable, the member should round down to the nearest quotable price. Stock prices are expected to decrease by the dividend amount when shares trade ex-dividend, since paying out a dividend reduces the cash held by the company.

75. **D)** A member that is party to a networking arrangement must tell new customers that the member—not the financial institution—is providing brokerage services. It must also disclose that transacted securities are not insured by the FDIC; securities are not deposits of the financial institution, nor are they guaranteed by the financial institution; and that

ANSWER KEY 111

securities are subject to investment risks that may include the loss of funds invested.

76. **B)** Complex portfolios may carry risk that is not characterized by the amount of cash required to construct the portfolio. As a result, many broker-dealers give certain customers the ability to post margin based on the overall risk exposure of the portfolio rather than on the market value of its constituent positions. Portfolio margin is especially useful for derivatives traders whose hedges offset the risks of other positions in the portfolio.

77. **C)** Listed stock options in the United States are physically settled. This involves delivery of shares rather than delivery of a cash amount. The risk characteristics and margin requirements for physical settlement are different from those for cash settlement. Cash settlement is used for certain index options and other instruments but not for options on single names or exchange-traded funds (ETFs). Note that settlement style is different from exercise style; a physically settled option can be American or European.

78. **A)** A revenue bond is a municipal debt instrument that uses cash flow from a specific project to pay for itself. An industrial development bond is a municipal debt instrument that finances a private company's project using the backing of a state or municipality. Option A meets both criteria: it is an industrial development bond insofar as the city raises money to build infrastructure for the direct benefit of a private company, and the debt is backed by the proceeds of the project.

    Option D may indirectly benefit a private company, but there is no revenue component, and it does not describe an industrial development bond because no private company is involved. Option C is backed by the full faith and credit of the municipality, so it describes a general obligation bond and not a revenue bond. Option B describes a revenue bond, not an industrial development bond.

79. **A)** Traditionally, the dividing line for an investment-grade bond versus a speculative-grade bond is established using a rating from a credit-rating agency. In the case of S&P Global Ratings, bonds rated BBB- or better are considered to be "investment grade," while bonds rated BB+ or worse are considered to be "speculative grade." Bond H was issued at a high coupon yield, but its credit rating is superior to that of Bond K. Usually, Bond H is described as "investment grade" due to its BBB rating, and Bond K is described as "speculative grade" due to its B rating.

80. **C)** Return on equity is a profitability ratio that describes how much money the company makes in a year relative to its assets minus liabilities.

81. **C)** A wash sale is a transaction that replaces a position closed at a loss within the past 30 days with a "substantially identical" position. The purpose of the wash-sale rule is to prevent taxpayers from artificially deducting capital losses. Eliminate Option D because it falls outside of the 30-day window. Eliminate Options A and B because they do not establish substantially identical positions to the long shares sold by the customer. Option A would take the customer short EF stock, and Option B would have a similarly bearish directional exposure. Only Option C would establish a substantially identical bullish position in EF stock within the 30-day wash-sale window.

82. **B)** The term *iron in an option* strategy means that it is composed of both calls and puts. An iron condor is similar to an iron butterfly in that each structure involves 2 calls and 2 puts. An iron condor is structured on four strikes, but an iron butterfly is structured upon three strikes, with the middle strike carrying two contracts. A condor is to a butterfly what a strangle is to a straddle; they have similar risk profiles, but the middle strike is broken out into two.

    One way to think of an iron condor is as two concentric strangles, with the narrower strangle traded in the opposite direction of the wider one. In this case, the iron condor is Option B. It can be interpreted as a short XYZ Sep 15/30 strangle traded against a long XYZ Sep 20/25 strangle.

83. **C)** Open interest reflects the number of contracts outstanding as of the end of the prior trading session. If the open interest is 4,322, if no other trades of the XYZ Nov 40 puts take place on the day of the trade described, and if neither party to that trade of 10,000 contracts

had an existing position in the option, then the open interest for the following day should reflect the existing 4,322 contracts plus the new trade of 10,000 contracts. Open interest would total 14,322 in the next day's trading session.

84. **B)** The premium collected from the sale of the put is incorporated into the cost basis of the shares. Since the shares are put to the option seller at the strike price of $30.00 and the option seller already received $4.00 in option premium when opening the position, the option seller's cost basis for the assigned shares is $26.00.

85. **C)** Section 3(a)(35) of the Securities Exchange Act of 1934 defines "investment discretion" over an account as either (a) being authorized to make transaction decisions, (b) making transaction decisions even though someone else is responsible for those decisions, or (c) exercising influence over transactions in any other way that the SEC determines, by rule, to be "investment discretion."

86. **B)** Brokerage firms must provide to FINRA short-interest data for customers and proprietary accounts twice monthly, on a per-security basis. In the case of exchange-traded stocks, listing exchanges disseminate this information to investors. In the case of over-the-counter stocks, FINRA publishes this information on its website.

87. **C)** "Regular way" for an option transaction is T + 1, but an option exercise is a transaction of the underlier, not a transaction of the option. So in this case, "regular way" refers to standard T + 2 settlement for US equity securities, as reflected in Option C. A standard T + 2 settlement timeline applies to stocks and exchange-traded funds (ETFs) whether a round lot of SPY trades directly on an exchange or via the exercise of an option. This settlement time was shortened from T + 3 in 2017. The fact that the underlier is an ETF and not a single-name equity security is not relevant.

88. **D)** A straddle is always worth more than a put with the same underlier, strike, and maturity. This is because the straddle includes that put plus a call whose value is always positive. The put in Option C can be eliminated because the Oct straddle in Option D is worth strictly more. All else being equal, a longer-dated option is worth more than a shorter-dated option, so between three straddles of the same underlier and strike but with different maturity, the longest-dated straddle is worth the most. The Oct 30-strike straddle has more time value than either the Aug or Sep 30-strike straddle, so Option D is correct.

89. **A)** Regulation S-P requires privacy policies and practices to be communicated to customers initially and annually. The regulation distinguishes between "consumers," "customers," and "former customers." Apart from stipulating that policy notices be provided to customers annually, Regulation S-P establishes opt-out policies, limits on information sharing, and exceptions thereof.

90. **B)** Eurobonds are named for the currency of denomination, so a eurodollar bond is denominated in dollars no matter who issues it or where it is held. A euroyen bond is denominated in yen, and a eurosterling bond is denominated in pounds sterling. Though a eurodollar bond is denominated in dollars, it is issued neither in the United States nor in the issuer's country of domicile.

91. **D)** Buyers pay the best offer; sellers receive the best bid. To buy the QRS Jan 30/50 call spread, one must buy the QRS Jan 30 call for $12.60 and sell the QRS Jan 50 call at $3.40. This results in a net premium debit of $9.20. The breakeven is located at the spot price where the intrinsic value of the call spread is equal to the premium, or $39.20.

92. **A)** The nominal, or coupon, yield is often much greater for a junk bond than for an investment-grade bond. Bonds with low credit quality are issued at a high yield to compensate investors for the risk involved in purchasing them. This would certainly be the case for a bond issued at par and rated Caa2. Most likely, the bond in question is now trading in the market at a substantial premium because buyers are willing to accept a lower yield for a more secure investment. There is no call provision for the bond, so Option D can be ignored.

93. **D)** The options trader's position results in two offsetting physical settlements at Oct expiry. She exercises the long call of the straddle to

buy 100 TUV shares for $400 and sells 100 TUV shares at $420 upon assignment of the short call of the call spread. The proceeds from these exercise transactions equal $20.00 per share, or $2,000 in total. They offset, leaving no TUV share position. The other two contracts, a long TUV Oct 400 put and a long TUV Oct 440 call, lapse. The options trader's profit equals the $2,000 proceeds from these transactions minus the net premium paid initially for the options structure. The options trader paid a net premium of $1,820 for the straddle and call spread, so her profit is $180 ($2,000 − $1,820 = $180).

94. **C)** Tenancy in common is a form of concurrent estate that generally has no rights of survivorship. Charlie's stake is transferable without the consent of the others who hold an ownership interest, and it will not automatically be absorbed by Ahmad and/or Brianna if Charlie passes away. Contrast this with a joint tenancy, which includes a right of survivorship.

95. **B)** The put in Option A has $3.00 of intrinsic value. The call spread in Option B has $5.00 of intrinsic value. The straddle in Option C has $1.00 of intrinsic value. The put butterfly in Option D has $3.00 of intrinsic value. Comparing these figures, it is clear that the call spread in Option B has the greatest intrinsic value. Note that there is not always a direct relationship between option value and intrinsic value; the straddle in Option C is worth far more than the call spread in Option B because the straddle has an unbounded maximum payoff and the call spread is limited to a maximum payoff of $5.00 minus the premium paid.

96. **B)** Yield to maturity is difficult to calculate in the absence of a fixed maturity date. In such cases, Rule 10b-10 of the Securities Exchange Act of 1934 waives the usual requirement for transaction confirmations to disclose the yield to maturity for a debt security.

97. **B)** The EFGH Aug 800 call is the only option that can be considered in-the-money when EFGH is trading at $860. The Jan 800 put and Oct 900 call are out-of-the-money. The Dec 860 call is at the money.

98. **C)** Regulation A enables public offering registration exemptions for small issues. Tier 1 exemptions are limited to $20 million in a 12-month period and have fewer requirements than Tier 2 exemptions, which are limited to $75 million in a 12-month period.

99. **C)** All three of the butterflies in the portfolio expire in March. The maximum payout of a long butterfly is achieved at its middle strike upon expiry, while the maximum payout of a short butterfly is achieved beyond the range of its strikes upon expiry. Both long butterflies in the portfolio are centered upon a middle strike of 70, and this strike falls outside of the range of the strikes of the short butterfly. Thus, the point of maximum payout is achieved if ABC stock closes at $70.00 upon Mar expiry. The spot price of ABC stock is immaterial.

100. **A)** In general, Rule 100 of Regulation M defines the restricted period as beginning 5 days before pricing of the offering. However, for securities where the average daily trading volume exceeds $100,000 and the issuer has a public float beyond $25 million, the restricted period begins 1 business day before pricing of the offering.

101. **B)** Systematic risk means overall market exposure. The long-only strategy (Option B) inherently carries systematic risk. If equity valuations fall market-wide due to factors beyond the scope of a particular sector, that sector's stocks will generally fall too. Merger arbitrage strategies carry some exposure to extreme changes in equity valuations. But price action of companies in special situations tends to be insulated from systematic risk and more connected to the terms of the merger deal. Market-neutral quantitative strategies minimize systematic risk. Capital structure arbitrage may have systematic exposure, but its nature as a spread between different securities of the same issuer tends to mitigate risk.

102. **B)** The market maker lost money on the put options and made money on the stock hedge. To determine the amount of his loss, subtract the hedge profit from the put loss. The stock hedge made 250,000 multiplied by $6.50, or $1,625,000. The put options have $6.30 of intrinsic value and $0.30 of time value, for a total premium of $6.60. Subtracting $2.55 from $6.60, multiplying the difference by 5,000, and multiplying again by the 100 contract multiplier results in an options

loss of $2,025,000. The total loss is therefore $400,000.

103. **C)** Consider the three Mar put contracts one by one. The investor can buy 100 STU Mar 50 puts for $80,000, and they would be worth $200,000 with STU stock at $30. She can alternatively buy 200 STU Mar 45 puts for the same premium outlay, and they would be worth $300,000 with STU stock at $30. Finally, she can buy 400 STU Mar 40 puts, and they would be worth $400,000 with STU stock at $30. Comparing these three contracts shows that the STU Mar 40 put provides the most protection if STU stock trades at $30 upon expiry.

104. **A)** According to FINRA Rule 11870, when a customer asks the receiving member (here, Brokerage B) to transfer securities held at a different FINRA member, both members must carry out the transfer. Only the customer's authorization is needed.

105. **A)** Unlike a tenancy in common arrangement, the ownership stake of a deceased stakeholder in a joint tenancy account stays with the remaining stakeholders. Even though Robert's will leaves his estate to Thomas, Susan retains Robert's stake in the joint tenancy account in the event of Robert's death.

106. **B)** Short selling of shares is not permitted in a cash account. Tiana can only exercise as many put contracts as she owns shares of ABC stock. The underlier of each ABC Apr 88 put contract is a round lot of 100 shares of ABC stock. Tiana cannot exercise eight contracts; doing so would require her to sell 2 ABC shares short. However, she can exercise seven contracts, leaving her with 98 shares of ABC stock and eight ABC Apr 88 put contracts.

107. **D)** Options A and B can be eliminated; due to the time value of options, the April strategies will be worth strictly less than their same-strike counterparts that expire 1 month later in May. Between the BCD May 70/80 strangle and the BCD May 70 straddle, the straddle is worth more. Both of the May strategies contain a BCD May 70 put, but the straddle contains a BCD May 70 call that is worth strictly more than the BCD May 80 call of the strangle.

108. **D)** A trade-through is a violation of Regulation NMS. It occurs when a trade is executed at a worse price than the best available price. The National Best Bid and Offer (NBBO) reflects the best prices at which one can respectively sell or buy a given security. So trades consummated within its confines are not considered to be trade-through violations.

109. **A)** US law permits soft dollar arrangements whereby customers overpay for commissions, as long as the services received in return are believed in good faith to be commensurate with the additional cost. This practice has been described as "paying up" for services and research.

110. **C)** A firm quote obligates the market maker to trade at the displayed price, and the market maker's failure to honor such a trade may be considered backing away. Quotations that are made without the promise of this obligation are described as indicative, subject, nominal, or qualified. Quotations that are not firm can be useful as guidelines to understand the market context for a given security.

111. **C)** Funds cannot be kept in a retirement account indefinitely. Holders of certain retirement accounts who turn 70 1/2 in 2020 or later must take their first required minimum distribution by April 1 of the year after reaching 72. For an account holder born in 1952, the relevant date is April 1, 2025. Roth IRAs are exempt from this requirement until after the account holder passes away.

112. **D)** Before the account holder can begin using Account 12345 as something other than an error account, its designation must be changed. According to FINRA Rule 4515, no change in account name or designation may take place unless a registered principal of the member approves. This approval, and the essential facts used by the registered principal to make the determination, must be recorded in writing before execution of any trade under the new account name or designation.

113. **C)** Inventory turnover ratio is a measure of cost of goods sold (COGS) versus inventory. The electronics retailer's gross margin of 50% means that her cost of goods sold was $160 million, or

half of the sales revenue number. This is four times the electronics retailer's average inventory figure of $40 million.

114. **B)** The Trust Indenture Act of 1939 supplemented the Securities Act of 1933 by establishing a requirement for certain debt issues to include trust indentures that formalize the terms and provisions of the debt. The Trust Indenture Act also placed greater obligations on trustees, improving the capacity of bondholders to take collective action against the issuer.

115. **C)** In the over-the-counter (OTC) credit market, credit traders in the United States tend to quote investment-grade bonds in terms of yield spread to a benchmark government security. In contrast, high-yield (junk) bonds are quoted in terms of dollar price. For example, a 30-year bond issued by a major telecommunications company may be offered at "+23" by a dealer, meaning 23 basis points above the yield to maturity of a corresponding 30-year Treasury bond.

116. **B)** Edwin's profit is the sum of the option premium collected and the profit from his short stock position. The option premium he collected is $410 multiplied by 6, or $2,460. The profit from his short stock position, sold at $22.10 and covered for $22.00 when the options are assigned, is 600 multiplied by $0.10, or $60.00. Edwin's total profit is $2,520, and he is left with no position in DEF.

117. **A)** All the options are put spreads that mature on the same date. Between two same-maturity put spreads of the same long strike, the one with greater strike width between the long put and short put is always worth more. Its greater payoff potential is reflected by a lesser premium collected from selling a lower put. Separately, between two same-maturity put spreads of the same strike width and differing strikes, the one struck higher is always worth more due to its greater likelihood of being in-the-money. The put spread in Option A has a greater strike width than Options B and C, which share a long strike with Option A. Furthermore, Option A is struck higher than Option D, which has the same strike width as Option A.

118. **D)** An SPX option contract is a cash-settled European option whose underlier is the S&P 500 Index. SPX options have global trading hours, allowing them to be traded at most hours during the week. SPY options are physically settled, and they are generally American-style contracts. Their underlier is the SPY exchange-traded fund (ETF), which tracks the S&P 500 but is about an order of magnitude smaller than the SPX Index. SPY options trade until just after the close of the regular trading session.

119. **C)** Whether preferred stock is participating or nonparticipating, it entitles the holder to a preferential liquidation payment that is superior to common stock in the capital structure. However, participating preferred stock also gets a share of the common stock equity payout. If there is no money left over for common shareholders after liquidation, then on balance there may be no difference between the value of participating and nonparticipating preferred shares. However, if the liquidation proceeds are sufficient to provide a payout to common shareholders, then participating preferred stock is worth more than nonparticipating preferred stock (all else being equal).

120. **B)** Barbara's loss on each share is $26.00, amounting to a loss of $2,600 on 100 shares. She paid $300 total for the put spread. The put spread is worth its maximum payout of $1,000 with UVW stock trading at $80.00, and the physical settlements of the short put and long put cancel out to leave no shares in her account. Barbara's gain on the put spread is $700, resulting in a net portfolio loss of $1,900.

121. **B)** Xavier's position can be thought of as a long JKL Dec 80 call alongside a JKL Sep 50/60 risk reversal. The Sep 50/60 risk reversal expires worthless, for a gain of the $2 premium collected initially. The Dec 80 call has no intrinsic value and $11 of time value, for a total of $11 premium upon Sep expiry and a loss of $1 versus the premium paid for the Dec 80 call initially. Xavier made $2 on the risk reversal and lost $1 on the call. Using the 100 multiplier, he made a total of $100 as of Sep expiry on his JKL position ($200 − $100 = $100).

122. **B)** Treasury stock is stock that was issued to shareholders and then reacquired by the

issuer. Share buyback programs are believed to return value to shareholders because the issuer purchases stock in the open market, reducing the number of outstanding shares and thus increasing earnings per share.

123. **A)** When interest rates fall, companies with callable bonds outstanding may be able to refinance that debt at a more favorable rate. This is not possible with a bullet bond because those are not callable. A put provision may only be exercised by the bondholder, so the issuer is powerless to use a put provision to effect early redemption. Calls with make-whole provisions provide the bondholder with compensation of the time value of the accelerated cash flows, so from the issuer's perspective make-whole call provisions are less attractive for early redemption than calls without make-whole provisions.

124. **B)** The SPX Index option does not affect the short notional. SPX options are not physically settled; they are settled versus the price of a basket of stocks, so no single underlying security can be delivered upon settlement. The parity value of the option is determined using a settlement price and is delivered in cash to the long holder of the option. A 5% rally of a $600,000 short position changes the position notional to $630,000. (A rally registers as a loss for Juana in this context.)

125. **D)** No member promoting a day-trading strategy may open a customer account without furnishing the Day-Trading Risk Disclosure Statement to the customer, per FINRA Rule 2270.

126. **C)** Fiduciary duty can be broken down into two categories: care and loyalty. Duty of care includes avoiding waste when executing transactions, advising on and monitoring positions and activities throughout a customer relationship, and providing advice in the customer's best interest. Duty of loyalty includes full and fair disclosure of conflicts of interest and informed consent regarding those conflicts. Profitability is an important objective for investment firms and retail investors alike, but failure to achieve profitability is not a breach of fiduciary duty.

127. **A)** This strangle has two break-even levels in the price of CDEF stock: $37 and $73. If the stock closes outside of that range upon Aug expiry, the position will reflect a loss. Only the price in Option A falls outside of the range of $37 and $73.

128. **B)** ABC stock is consolidating in the range between $85 and $90 after a substantial rally in the past year. The fact that the 6-month moving average is similar to the 3-month moving average indicates that the average price of ABC is remaining stable. The low volatility implied by the options market suggests that the price does not move too far away from this average.

129. **A)** This question describes a situation often seen when manufacturing processes mature: margin expansion due to lower costs. FGH Widgets Incorporated is somehow able to sell the same number of widgets at the same price as always, but its unit costs go down and its fixed costs remain stable. The company's gross profit increases. Fixed costs remain the same, so the increase in gross profit also results in increased operating income.

130. **A)** Selling securities short without having located borrow is called "naked shorting." This is an illegal practice. Naked shorting promises the buyer delivery of a security that the seller neither owns nor can find. The US credit market is an over-the-counter market, but participants in that market are still required to locate borrow before effecting a short sale.

131. **C)** The acronym *ACATS* stands for Automated Customer Account Transfer Service. This system was built to make it easier to transfer securities between accounts at different firms. Its benefits include standardized procedures, faster settlements, and reduced costs. Not all holdings are eligible to be transferred via ACATS, but those that are include stocks, bonds, annuities, options, mutual funds, and unit investment trusts.

132. **C)** Premium is equal to time value plus intrinsic value. The put in the DEF Nov 65 straddle has an intrinsic value of $4, and the call has no intrinsic value. Subtraction of the straddle's $4 intrinsic value from its $18 premium gives a time value of $14.

133. **D)** FINRA Rule 11892 establishes threshold criteria to decide if a transaction in an exchange-listed security is clearly erroneous. During market hours, if the reference price is $25.00 or below, the threshold is 10%; for a reference price above $25.00 but not higher than $50.00, the threshold is 5%; for a reference price above $50.00, the threshold is 3%. Outside of market hours, these thresholds double. Barring extenuating circumstances, prints beyond the threshold are considered to be clearly erroneous. For example, a $43.00 print of a stock that last traded $40.00 might be considered erroneous intraday, but not after hours. (Different criteria apply to multi-stock events.)

134. **C)** Statutory voting allows a shareholder to vote each of her shares for one candidate. In contrast, cumulative voting allows a shareholder to vote each of her shares for one candidate for each seat available. If Sonia so desires, she can vote for her favorite candidate 700 times for each of the three seats, for a total of 2,100 ballots cast to that candidate.

135. **C)** Named for Green Shoe Mfg., a greenshoe option allows the underwriter to offer a greater allotment of shares in an initial public offering. This option grants the underwriter the ability to access more inventory without carrying price risk on the over-allotment. Greenshoe options are limited to 15% of the number of securities offered.

www.ingramcontent.com/pod-product compliance
Lightning Source LLC
Chambersburg PA
CBHW080345170426
43194CB00014B/2695